LYNN BEDFORD HALL

THE BEST OF BISCUITS & BREADS

LYNN BEDFORD HALL

THE BEST OF BISCUITS & BREADS

PHOTOGRAPHY BY ANTHONY JOHNSON

STRUIK

Struik Publishers (Pty) Ltd
(a member of The Struik Publishing Group (Pty) Ltd)
Cornelis Struik House
80 McKenzie Street
Cape Town 8001

Reg. No.: 54/00965/07

First published in 1993
Second impression 1994

Editor: Elizé Lübbe
Designer: Petal Palmer
Photographer: Anthony Johnson
Stylist: Vo Pollard
Illustrator: Tobie Beele

Typesetting by BellSet, Cape Town
Reproduction by Unifoto (Pty) Ltd, Cape Town
Printed and bound by Tien Wah Press (Pte.) Ltd, Singapore

ISBN 1-86825-318-X

CONTENTS

ACKNOWLEDGEMENTS

Apart from the help I received from my family, who were eternally being called upon to taste and pronounce judgement, I also wish to thank Linda de Villiers of Struik Publishers for her enthusiasm, advice and professional handling of the manuscript, and Marje Hemp, who initiated the whole project and was always there to guide and encourage. A very special acknowledgement goes to Vo Pollard, whose remarkable flair for baking and styling is evident in the stunning photographs by Anthony Johnson. The credit for designing goes to Petal Palmer, whose enthusiasm and hard work meant so much, while Elizé Lübbe's meticulous editing completed the fine work done by this talented team. I am grateful, as well, to the Defy Company, who have so generously sponsored me with a new stove, to SA Philips (Pty) Ltd for presenting me with a brand new mixer, and to the editor of the *Sunday Times* for permission to use many of my recipes which have appeared in the *Magazine*.

The photographer and publishers are grateful to the following people and companies in Cape Town for the loan of crockery, fabric and furniture:

Collector's Corner
The Cape Heritage Shop
China Rose, Claremont
Interior Art, Observatory
Biggie Best, Claremont
Strippers, Wynberg
Stuttafords Greatermans, Claremont
Bric-a-Brac Lane, Claremont

FOREWORD

This book is the result of a very long baking affair. For months I have mixed and kneaded, creamed and rolled, proved and cut, and it has left me – not only a little floury – but also convinced that home-baking should definitely be put back on the culinary map.

There are, however, so many good biscuits and breads on the market these days, that many people have lost the urge to make their own. This is a pity, because not only is baking both relaxing and enjoyable, but nothing out of a packet can match the nose-twitching aroma of freshly baked bread, scones and muffins.

Bread-baking, in particular, can become an addictive pastime. Kneading is wonderfully therapeutic and gets rid of a lot of aggression on the days when you're feeling uptight.

Baking biscuits and rusks, quick breads, scones and muffins can be equally satisfying and is a means to endless creativity. For example, in certain recipes I have substituted wholewheat flour for some of the cake flour. This does mean that the end product will be a little heavier and different in texture from the refined versions, but rather more wholesome and in line with the present swing to less processed ingredients. You will probably also notice that I have cut down a little on sugar and salt, proving that one can jiggle recipes to adapt to one's own tastes and convictions, and I am sure you will find yourself adding many personal touches to my ideas.

In most recipes you will not have to use a scale. Quantities are such that they can easily be measured with a metric cup or spoon, and even when butter is used, the recipes almost always require a block simply to be cut into convenient halves or quarters.

I have, without exception, used extra large eggs, and I suggest you do the same, else you might end up with too little liquid and, therefore, a different result.

For creaming and mixing most biscuits and sweet loaves, I have used a hand-held Philips three-speed electric beater. I cannot guarantee the same results if you try creaming with a wooden spoon. Using an electric beater is quick, easy and thorough. However, I have rarely used the dough hooks for bread, simply because I think it is important to develop a personal relationship with your dough. If you feel and knead it with your hands it becomes, in today's idiom, user-friendly, and you will soon learn to tell when the right consistency has been reached.

I hope, with this book, to help define the trend back to home cooking. Even if it is only on special, less pressurized days, homecooks all over are definitely displaying a predilection for presenting their families with bakes that didn't start out pre-wrapped in a trolley. I've done it, and so can you, and while test-baking for this book there were many occasions on which I called my family to come and peer in through the glass oven door to watch whatever it was rising, spreading and browning. Which proves that baking can become a communal experience and when the results are good, the reward is a companionable sharing.

And finally, all that is left to be said is to wish you the best of baking, and happy munching!

Lynn Bedford Hall

BISCUITS & COOKIES

The Updated Soetkoekie

Granny used mutton fat and red bolus and left her soetkoekie dough to stand overnight, followed by a long session of rolling and cutting out little circles with a glass. Granny had lots of time, and would doubtless have disapproved of these easy spice 'n slice cookies, using everyday ingredients – but do try them – they're a super alternative.

300 ml cake flour or white bread flour
300 ml brown bread flour
5 ml baking powder
1 ml salt
2 ml bicarbonate of soda
5 ml ground mixed spice
5 ml ground cinnamon
1 ml ground cloves
2 ml ground ginger
125 g soft butter
125 ml sugar
125 ml light brown sugar
1 egg
30 ml sweet sherry

Sift both flours with baking powder, salt, bicarbonate of soda and spices. Return any bran left in sifter. Cream butter and slowly add both sugars, beating well. Beat egg with sherry and beat into butter mixture with 5 ml of the flour mixture, then mix in rest of flour mixture to make a soft dough. Shape into two 3 cm-diameter sausages. Wrap in greaseproof paper and chill for about 1 hour. Using a sharp knife, slice into 4 mm-thick rounds and place on oiled baking trays, leaving room for spreading. Bake at 160 °C for 15 minutes, then remove to wire racks to cool and crisp.
Makes 70

Bright and dainty little Coconut Cherry Winks (page 19) and crisp Lemon Sesame Snaps.

Nut and Oat Cookies

Simple, old-fashioned buttery biscuits.

250 g soft butter
250 ml sugar
5 ml vanilla essence
1 egg, beaten
500 ml cake flour
50 ml cornflour
1 ml salt
10 ml baking powder
250 ml rolled oats
200 ml finely chopped pecan nuts

Cream butter, sugar and vanilla. Add egg and mix well. Sift flour, cornflour, salt and baking powder and add. Mix until combined and then add oats and nuts. Knead with your hands until mixture forms a ball. Pinch off small pieces, roll into balls, and place on oiled baking trays. Press down lightly with a fork and bake at 180 °C on middle shelf of oven for 20 minutes. Cool on wire rack.
Makes 48

Brownies

There are several versions of this well-known American favourite; this one is like a very light, thinly crusted chocolate cake.

3 eggs
200 ml white sugar
50 ml light brown sugar
100 g dark chocolate, broken up
125 g butter
300 ml cake flour
5 ml baking powder
1 ml salt
250 ml chopped walnuts or pecan nuts
5 ml vanilla essence

Beat eggs and sugars together until thick and pale. Melt chocolate with butter over very low heat. Beat into egg mixture. Sift flour, baking powder and salt, add to egg mixture and stir until combined. Stir in nuts and vanilla. Pour into oiled 26 x 21 cm baking tin and bake at 180 °C for 35 minutes until just firm and starting to crack round the edges. Be careful not to overbake. Cut into squares and leave to cool in tin. These brownies keep well.
Makes 36

HINT
- *Keep biscuits crisp by storing them in airtight containers with a sprinkling of sugar between the layers.*

Lemon Sesame Snaps

Deliciously crisp, brown biscuits. Toasting brings out the flavour of sesame seeds: spread them out on a large baking tray and place in oven, either preheated, or when you turn it on prior to baking. Remove when golden brown, watching carefully as they burn easily.

125 g soft butter
2 ml vanilla essence
100 ml castor sugar
10 ml finely grated lemon rind
25 ml honey
150 ml white bread flour
1 ml salt
2 ml bicarbonate of soda
150 ml wholewheat flour
100 ml toasted sesame seeds

Cream butter, vanilla, sugar, lemon rind and honey. Sift white bread flour with salt and bicarbonate of soda. Mix into creamed mixture, then add wholewheat flour and sesame seeds. Combine well to a soft dough. Shape into a ball, pinch off small pieces, roll into balls and place on oiled baking trays, leaving room for spreading. Press down with tines of a fork, making a criss-cross pattern, and bake at 180 °C for 12 minutes. Leave on tray for 1 minute to crisp, then transfer to wire rack to cool.
Makes 30

Basic Butter Biscuits

The old-fashioned cookie, simple and good. Make several batches and flavour them in a variety of ways – they're very quick to mix with the help of a hand-held electric beater.

125 g soft butter
200 ml castor sugar
1 egg, lightly beaten
5 ml vanilla essence
500 ml white bread flour
5 ml cream of tartar
2 ml bicarbonate of soda

Cream butter and sugar until light, then add egg and vanilla and beat. Sift the dry ingredients and add. Mix to a soft dough and then shape into a ball with your hands. Pinch off walnut-sized pieces and place them on an oiled or non-stick baking tray, leaving room for spreading. Press down lightly with the tines of a fork and bake at 180 °C for about 12 minutes, or until pale beige in colour. Remove to wire rack to cool completely. Store in an airtight container.
Makes 30

VARIATIONS

Coffee Pecan Butter Biscuits
Substitute light brown sugar for the castor sugar. Beat egg lightly with 15 ml instant coffee granules and the vanilla essence, until coffee has dissolved. Add 100 ml finely chopped pecan nuts to the dough and top each cookie with a pecan piece.

Lemon Peel Butter Biscuits
Cream butter and sugar with 5 ml finely grated lemon rind. Use only 250 ml white bread flour when sifting, then add 250 ml wholewheat flour and 75 ml finely chopped mixed peel. Top each cookie with a dried sultana.

Chocolate Butter Biscuits
Sift 10 ml cocoa powder with the dry ingredients and add 50 g grated dark chocolate to the dough. Press a Morsel into the top of each biscuit. Chocolate Morsels are sold in 250 g packets at most leading supermarkets.

Munchies

Knobbly cookies, containing wholesome ingredients.

125 ml self-raising flour
5 ml ground cinnamon
250 ml wholewheat flour
200 ml sugar
150 ml oil
2 eggs
200 ml rolled oats
250 ml fruit cake mix
125 ml desiccated coconut

Sift together the self-raising flour and cinnamon, then mix in wholewheat flour. Whisk together sugar, oil and eggs. Add to dry ingredients together with oats, fruit and coconut. Mix very well to a soft dough. Push large teaspoonfuls off onto oiled baking trays and bake at 180 °C for 18 minutes. Using a spatula, transfer to wire racks to cool and crisp. Store the cookies in an airtight container, with a sprinkling of sugar between the layers.
Makes 40

Coconut Lemon Crispies

Pale gold, crunchy little discs, made with oil instead of butter.

100 ml oil
200 ml castor sugar
7 ml finely grated lemon rind
1 egg
500 ml white bread flour
2 ml baking powder
pinch salt
250 ml desiccated coconut
extra castor sugar

> NOTE
> • *Butter biscuits should be baked on the middle shelf of the oven to avoid browned bottoms, therefore it is best to bake them in relays.*

Place oil, sugar and lemon rind in a deep rather than a wide mixing bowl, and beat very well. Add egg and beat until mixture is creamy and yellow. Sift together flour, baking powder and salt, add to creamed mixture and mix well, then beat in coconut. Roll into balls and press flat between palms. Dip tops in extra castor sugar and place on oiled baking trays, sugar side up, leaving room for spreading. Bake at 180 °C for 15 minutes until just browning around the edges. Cool on wire rack.
Makes 30

Cookie Press Biscuits

This dough keeps its shape well and may be used for any design, but is particularly attractive pressed into daisy shapes with half a glacé cherry in the centre. Alternatively, sprinkle with cinnamon-sugar (mix 2 ml ground cinnamon with 5 ml castor sugar), or top with finely chopped almonds, pressed in lightly. The dough may also be flavoured with grated lemon or orange rind, or the biscuits may be sandwiched together using vanilla butter icing, as in the recipe for Chocolate Logs on page 21.

125 g soft butter
125 ml castor sugar
1 egg
5 ml vanilla essence
450 ml cake flour
50 ml cornflour
pinch salt

Cream butter and sugar. Beat egg with vanilla and add. Mix well and then add flour sifted with cornflour and salt. Combine well to a soft dough and then press into a ball with your hands, rather like shortbread. Fill the cookie press and press out onto lightly oiled baking trays, not too close because, although the mixture does not contain any raising agent, the biscuits spread slightly as the butter melts. Bake at 200 °C for 12-15 minutes until pale beige in colour. Cool on wire rack.
Makes 30-36

FROM THE BACK: *Chocolate Cookies; Coconut Lemon Crispies; Namib Knobs; Cookie Press Biscuits.*

Chocolate Cookies

There are many versions of this favourite American cookie. Chips usually retain their shape, while chopped chocolate melts in the baking.

125 g soft butter
60 ml light brown sugar
60 ml castor sugar
1 egg
2 ml vanilla essence
2 ml bicarbonate of soda
10 ml hot water
400 ml cake flour
pinch salt
10 ml cocoa powder
1 x 100 g slab dark chocolate
100-125 ml chopped walnuts or pecan nuts

Cream butter and both sugars until light. Beat egg with vanilla and add, mixing well. Stir in bicarbonate of soda dissolved in hot water. Sift in flour, salt and cocoa. Combine well. Chop chocolate in food processor and add together with nuts, mixing to a softish dough. Now either pinch off small balls and flatten between the palms before placing on oiled baking trays, or push off rough mounds from the tip of a teaspoon. Bake at 180 °C for 20 minutes. Leave to cool on a wire rack.

Makes 36

Namib Knobs

These crisp little cakes are stuffed with dates and very similar to mince pies in appearance.

PASTRY
500 ml cake flour (loosely measured)
50 ml cornflour
50 ml icing sugar
175 g butter
1 egg
2 ml vanilla essence
extra icing sugar

FILLING
250 g pitted dates, chopped
5 ml lemon juice
50 ml water
75 ml chopped walnuts

First make the filling. Put dates, lemon juice and water into a small saucepan and heat gently until dates are soft enough to be mashed with a wooden spoon. Add nuts and set aside to cool.

Sift flour, cornflour and icing sugar. Rub in butter. Beat egg and vanilla and add. Mix well. Knead into a ball – do not add any liquid. Roll out thinly on a floured board and cut into 5-7 cm circles. Re-roll off-cuts until all the dough has been used. Place a heaped spoon of filling in the middle of each round, cover with a second round and seal edges with the tines of a fork. Prick each top twice. Place on oiled baking tray and bake at 180 °C for 18-20 minutes or until pale gold. Remove to wire rack and dredge with sifted icing sugar.

Makes 14

Coconut Currant Snaps

A typical cookie-jar biscuit, economical and easy.

125 g soft butter
200 ml castor sugar
1 egg
5 ml vanilla essence
500 ml self-raising flour
pinch salt
250 ml desiccated coconut
125 ml currants
extra castor sugar

Cream butter and sugar. Mix in egg beaten with vanilla. Sift flour with salt and add to creamed mixture together with coconut. Finally mix in currants. Knead to a ball, then pinch off small pieces and roll into balls. Press flat between the palms, dip tops in extra castor sugar and place on oiled baking trays, leaving room for spreading. Bake at 180 °C for 15 minutes until just beginning to brown. Cool on wire racks.
Makes 50

Melting Moments

Butter-rich cookies, rolled in crushed cereal before baking.

125 g soft butter
125 ml castor sugar
1 egg, lightly beaten
5 ml vanilla essence
400 ml self-raising flour
1 ml salt
250 ml All-Bran flakes or cornflakes, coarsely crushed

Cream butter and sugar. Add egg and vanilla and beat well. Sift flour with salt and add. Mix well to a soft ball. Pinch off small pieces, roll into balls and roll in crushed cereal. Arrange on oiled baking trays, leaving room for spreading, and press down lightly with a fork. Bake on middle shelf of oven at 180 °C for 15 minutes. Cool on wire rack.
Makes 30

Carrot and Coconut Jumbles

Big, chewy, wholesome – and so quick to make.

125 g butter
250 ml light brown sugar
250 ml wholewheat flour
250 ml cake flour
250 ml desiccated coconut
250 ml rolled oats
500 ml coarsely grated carrots
5 ml bicarbonate of soda
1 ml salt
10 ml ground cinnamon
2 ml ground nutmeg
125 ml sultanas or seedless raisins
2 eggs, lightly beaten
2 ml vanilla essence
125 ml oil

Cream butter and sugar. Add flours, coconut, oats, carrots, bicarbonate of soda, salt, spices and sultanas or raisins. Beat together eggs, vanilla and oil. Add to dry ingredients and mix very well – use an electric beater – mixture will eventually form a soft dough. Push heaped teaspoonfuls off onto lightly oiled baking trays, leaving room for spreading, and press down lightly with a fork. Bake at 180 °C for 20 minutes. Stand for 1 minute to crisp, then use a spatula to remove to wire racks to cool.
Makes 48

Wholewheat, Honey and Coconut Crisps

Caramel-coloured, crunchy biscuits – a top favourite.

125 g butter, melted
25 ml honey
100 ml light brown sugar
300 ml wholewheat flour
pinch salt
2 ml bicarbonate of soda
10 ml hot water
125 ml desiccated coconut
2 ml vanilla essence

Mix melted butter with honey, sugar, flour and salt. Add bicarbonate of soda dissolved in hot water. Mix in coconut and vanilla. Combine thoroughly until mixture forms a soft ball. Pinch off small pieces and roll into balls. Place on ungreased baking trays, leaving room for spreading. Press down lightly with a fork and then bake at 180 °C for 12-14 minutes until a rich brown colour. Cool on wire rack.
Makes 28

Florentines

A thin, lacy biscuit with dried fruit and nuts, coated with chocolate on one side.

60 g butter
60 ml castor sugar
25 ml sifted cake flour
100 ml chopped almonds
12 glacé cherries, chopped
50 ml sultanas, chopped
2 knobs preserved ginger, chopped
50 ml mixed peel, chopped
100 g dark chocolate

Cream butter and sugar well. Fold in flour. Add almonds and fruit. Spoon large teaspoonfuls, far apart, onto baking trays, preferably non-stick but otherwise oiled and dusted with cornflour. Flatten lightly with the back of a spoon. Bake at 180 °C for about 10 minutes or until browned with lacy edges. Remove from oven and, using a spoon, push lightly into neat circles. Using a spatula, remove carefully to wire rack to cool. Melt chocolate very gently over simmering water – do not allow it to get too hot – and spread evenly over flat side of each cooled biscuit. Run a fork through the chocolate as it hardens to make the characteristic wavy pattern. When cold and set, store in airtight container.
Makes 14

Coconut Almond Crisps

125 g soft butter
200 ml castor sugar
2 ml vanilla essence
1 egg, lightly beaten
500 ml self-raising flour
1 ml salt
200 ml desiccated coconut
125 ml finely chopped toasted almonds

Cream butter, sugar and vanilla until light. Add egg and beat. Sift in flour and salt and mix well. Add coconut and almonds and knead to a soft ball. Pinch off small pieces, roll into balls and place on oiled baking trays, leaving plenty of room for spreading. Press twice with a fork, making a criss-cross pattern, and bake at 180 °C for 20 minutes or until a deep beige colour. Cool on wire racks.
Makes 40

Vanilla Condensed Milk Drops

This easy recipe makes a large batch of crisp cookies, either plain or topped with cinnamon-sugar.

250 g soft butter
100 ml castor sugar
½ x 397 g can condensed milk
750 ml cake flour
10 ml baking powder
1 ml salt
5 ml vanilla essence

Cream butter and sugar. Beat in condensed milk. Sift flour with baking powder and salt and add to creamed mixture. Finally add vanilla and mix well to a soft dough. Push small mounds off the tip of a teaspoon onto oiled or non-stick baking tray. Flatten with a fork, in a criss-cross pattern. Sprinkle with cinnamon-sugar if preferred. Bake at 180 °C for 15 minutes or until just beginning to brown. Cool on wire rack.
Makes 54

FROM THE BACK: *Carrot and Coconut Jumbles; Melting Moments; Wholewheat, Honey and Coconut Crisps.*

FROM THE TOP: *Spiced Sultana Slices; All-Bran Crisps; Coconut Slices.*

One-Bowl Raisin-Bran Bars

250 ml self-raising flour
200 ml sugar
250 ml desiccated coconut
200 ml seedless raisins or sultanas
50 ml mixed peel
75 ml sunflower seeds
60 g soft butter, diced
100 ml oil
1 egg, beaten
250 ml All-Bran flakes
2 ml vanilla essence

Put ingredients in above order into large mixing bowl. Using an electric beater, beat very well until thoroughly combined. Spread evenly into a lightly oiled 21 x 21 cm baking tin. Bake on middle shelf of oven at 180 °C for about 30 minutes until firm and well browned. Cut into bars and cool in tin.
Makes 18 large bars

Sour Cream Spice Biscuits

250 g soft butter
5 ml ground cinnamon
5 ml ground mixed spice
1 ml grated nutmeg
500 ml light brown sugar
1 egg, lightly beaten
125 ml sour cream
4 x 250 ml cake flour
2 ml bicarbonate of soda
2 ml salt

Cream butter with spices. Slowly beat in sugar. Beat in egg and cream. Sift flour, bicarbonate of soda and salt. Add to creamed mixture and combine to a soft dough, then shape into a ball with your hands. Pinch off small pieces and roll into balls, flouring hands when necessary. Place on oiled baking trays and press down with fork, making a criss-cross pattern. Bake on middle shelf of oven at 180 °C for 15 minutes. Leave on a wire rack until cold.
Makes 72

Muesli and Wheat Germ Crisps

60 g soft butter, diced
60 ml oil
1 egg
2 ml vanilla essence or 5 ml grated orange rind
250 ml self-raising flour
200 ml sugar
2 ml salt
100 ml untoasted wheat germ
100 ml desiccated coconut
150 ml seedless raisins or sultanas
250 ml muesli

Put into bowl in above order and use an electric beater to beat very well until butter has dissolved and mixture can be kneaded into a ball with the hands. Pinch off pieces slightly larger than a walnut, set well apart on oiled baking trays and press down with the tines of a fork. Bake on middle shelf of oven at 180 °C for about 20 minutes until lightly browned. Use a spatula to remove to wire rack to cool and crisp.
Makes 30 large cookies

All-Bran Crisps

125 g soft butter
250 ml sugar
250 ml white bread flour
5 ml baking powder
pinch salt
2 ml bicarbonate of soda
5 ml ground mixed spice
1 egg
2 ml vanilla essence
250 ml All-Bran flakes
250 ml desiccated coconut
250 ml rolled oats

Cream butter and sugar until light. Sift flour, baking powder, salt, bicarbonate of soda and spice and add. Mix well, then add egg beaten with vanilla. When combined, stir in coarsely crushed All-Bran flakes, coconut and oats. Roll into small balls and place on oiled baking trays, leaving plenty of room for spreading. Press down with bottom of a glass and bake at 180 °C for about 20 minutes until browned. Cool on wire rack.
Makes 40

Spiced Pecan Crisps

125 g butter
250 ml light brown sugar
1 egg
2 ml vanilla essence
600 ml cake flour
2 ml baking powder
1 ml bicarbonate of soda
5 ml ground cinnamon
2 ml grated nutmeg
125 ml chopped pecan nuts

Cream butter with sugar until fluffy. Beat in egg and vanilla. Sift dry ingredients and add to creamed mixture, combining thoroughly. Lastly stir in pecan nuts. Form into sausages, wrap in greaseproof paper and freeze for about 45 minutes, until firm.

To bake, slice fairly thin and place on lightly oiled baking tray. Bake at 180 °C for 12-15 minutes, until pale golden brown. Cool on wire rack.
Makes about 54

Spiced Sultana Slices

The texture of these lies somewhere between a slab cake and a biscuit. They are made without either egg yolks or butter, and are baked in flat strips which are later cut into diagonal slices.

1 egg white
5 ml lemon juice
125 ml castor sugar
125 ml golden syrup
125 ml oil
750 ml cake flour
5 ml bicarbonate of soda
1 ml salt
5 ml ground ginger
5 ml ground mixed spice
2 ml grated nutmeg
250 ml sultanas

Whisk egg white, lemon juice, sugar, syrup and oil until thoroughly blended. Sift flour, bicarbonate of soda, salt and spices, and add slowly to first mixture, while beating. Stir in sultanas and mix to a dough. Roll into four 25 mm-diameter sausages. Place on oiled baking trays and press down lightly to flatten. Bake on middle shelf of oven at 180 °C for 18 minutes, or until nicely browned. Cool for a few minutes and then cut on the diagonal into slices about 2 cm thick. Cool on wire rack.
Makes 40

Easter Biscuits

These biscuits are perfect for lunch-boxes as they do not crumble.

550 ml cake flour
1 ml salt
5 ml baking powder
5 ml ground mixed spice
2 ml ground cinnamon
1 ml grated nutmeg
125 g soft butter
150 ml castor sugar
125 ml currants
60 ml chopped mixed peel
1 egg, lightly beaten
extra castor sugar

Sift flour, salt, baking powder and spices. Rub in butter. Stir in sugar, currants and peel. Add egg, mix to a dough and then shape into a ball. Do not add any liquid, just knead lightly until mixture holds together. Pat out on floured board and then roll gently with a rolling pin to flatten to about 1 cm thick. Cut out rounds with a fluted, 6 cm cutter and place on oiled baking trays. Bake at 180 °C for 12-15 minutes until lightly browned. Remove to wire rack, sprinkle with castor sugar and cool.
Makes 30-34

Coconut Slices

Once chilled, the biscuit dough is sliced into cookies in seconds, making refrigerator biscuits the quickest and easiest to prepare for the oven.

150 g soft butter
250 ml sugar
1 egg
5 ml vanilla essence
500 ml cake flour (half brown bread flour may be used)
1 ml salt
2 ml bicarbonate of soda
250 ml desiccated coconut

Cream butter and sugar until light. Add egg and vanilla and beat well. Sift flour with salt and bicarbonate of soda and mix into creamed mixture. Add coconut. Work into a ball and then divide into two 3 cm-diameter sausages. Wrap in greaseproof paper and chill for 1 hour. Using a sharp knife, cut into 6 mm slices and place fairly far apart on an ungreased baking tray. Bake at 160 °C on middle shelf of oven, for about 12 minutes. Cool on wire rack.
Makes about 60

Mocha Chocolate Logs

Dipped into melted chocolate and rolled in nuts, these are attractive little logs with the texture of shortbread.

20 ml instant coffee granules
20 ml water
250 g soft butter
125 ml castor sugar
5 ml vanilla essence
600 ml cake flour
125 ml cornflour
pinch salt
dark chocolate and finely chopped almonds

Dissolve coffee granules in water. Add to butter and sugar and cream until light. Add vanilla. Sift together flour, cornflour and salt, add to creamed mixture and beat to a soft dough – a hand-held electric beater may be used. Using a piping bag with a star-shaped nozzle, pipe 5 cm-long logs onto ungreased baking trays. Bake at 160 °C for 15-20 minutes until a pale golden brown. Stand on trays for a few minutes before removing to wire rack to cool. Melt the chocolate in small pot over hot water. Dip one end of each biscuit into the melted chocolate and then roll in nuts until coated. Return to wire rack to set.
Makes 48

Cinnamon Jam Biscuits

Quick to make and economical – a sure winner!

125 g soft butter
200 ml light brown sugar
1 egg, lightly beaten
250 ml white bread flour
5 ml bicarbonate of soda
1 ml salt
10 ml ground cinnamon
50 ml smooth apricot jam
250 ml wholewheat flour

Cream butter and sugar. Add egg and beat well. Sift white bread flour, bicarbonate of soda, salt and cinnamon and add to creamed mixture together with the jam. Mix well and then add wholewheat flour and combine to make a soft dough. Push little mounds off the tip of a teaspoon onto oiled baking trays, leaving room for spreading, and bake at 180 °C for 10 minutes or until lightly browned. Cool on wire rack. Store in airtight container, with a sprinkling of sugar between the layers.
Makes 40

Snickerdoodles

Soft and spicy.

250 g soft butter
250 ml sugar
2 eggs, lightly beaten
5 ml vanilla essence
750 ml white bread flour
75 ml cornflour
10 ml cream of tartar
5 ml bicarbonate of soda
1 ml salt
50 ml castor sugar
10 ml ground cinnamon
2 ml ground mixed spice

Cream butter and sugar. Add eggs and vanilla and beat until creamy. Sift flour, cornflour, cream of tartar, bicarbonate of soda and salt. Add to creamed mixture and mix to a soft dough. Pinch off walnut-sized pieces and roll into small balls. On a large plate mix castor sugar with spices. Roll each ball in this mixture, coating well, then place well apart on ungreased baking tray. Sprinkle any leftover sugar mixture over the tops, and press down lightly with back of fork. Bake at 180 °C for 15 minutes. Initially they will rise like top hats and then settle into disc shapes. Transfer to wire rack to cool.
Makes 48

Granny's Ginger Snaps

600 ml cake flour
250 ml castor sugar
2 ml bicarbonate of soda
2 ml ground mixed spice
1 ml salt
10 ml ground ginger
125 g soft butter
1 egg
25 ml thin honey
slivers of preserved ginger

Sift dry ingredients. Rub in butter. Beat egg and honey and mix into the dough, then knead into a ball. Do not add any more liquid. Pinch off walnut-sized pieces of dough, roll into balls and place on non-stick or oiled baking tray allowing plenty of room for spreading. Press a sliver of preserved ginger into the top of each, and bake at 160 °C for 20 minutes or until lightly browned. Remove to wire rack to cool.
Makes 30-36

Fruity Fridge Squares

250 g butter
4 x 250 ml icing sugar
2 eggs, beaten
1 packet Tennis biscuits, coarsely broken
250 ml desiccated coconut
5 ml vanilla essence
125 ml mixed peel
125 ml sultanas

Melt butter over low heat. Slowly blend in sifted icing sugar. Keeping heat very low, stir in eggs – on no account must the mixture boil or they will scramble. Add biscuits. Mix well, remove from stove and add remaining ingredients. Combine thoroughly, using a wooden spoon. Press flat into a shallow dish greased with soft margarine. Cool, and then chill before cutting into small squares. Store in refrigerator.
Makes 48

FROM THE TOP: *Mocha Chocolate Logs; Cinnamon Jam Biscuits; Fruity Fridge Squares; Granny's Ginger Snaps.*

Old-fashioned Jam Squares

A biscuit base spread with jam and a crumble topping – this recipe fills a large baking tray and is easily made using an electric beater.

250 g soft butter
250 ml sugar
2 eggs
5 ml vanilla essence
4 x 250 ml cake flour
15 ml baking powder
generous pinch salt
smooth apricot jam
icing sugar

Cream butter and sugar well. Beat eggs with vanilla, add, and mix well. Sift flour, baking powder and salt, beat into creamed mixture and mix well until mixture forms a soft ball that holds together. Pinch off two-thirds of dough and press and pat out evenly into lightly oiled 37 x 25 cm baking tray. Spread generously with jam. Using the coarse side of a grater, grate remaining dough over the top – don't press down, simply spread with a fork. (There is no need to chill the dough first. It should not stick if you run the grater under the tap now and then.) Bake on middle shelf of oven at 180 °C for about 35 minutes until golden brown. Cut into squares and leave to cool in tin. Sift a little icing sugar over before removing.
Makes 32

Old-fashioned Jam Squares; Coconut Macaroons; Coconut Cherry Winks and clove studded Almond Crescents.

Brown Sugar Cookies

The sort of crisp, buttery cookie my granny used to make to fill the cookie jar.

250 g soft butter
250 ml light brown sugar
1 egg, lightly beaten
5 ml vanilla essence
750 ml self-raising flour
pinch salt
quartered pecan nuts or glacé cherries (optional)

Using an electric beater, cream butter and sugar until light. Add egg and vanilla and beat. Add flour and salt and continue beating until very well combined, then shape into a soft, smooth ball with your hands. Pinch off small pieces and roll into balls the size of a large marble. Place on ungreased baking trays and press down with a fork in a criss-cross pattern. If using, gently press a quartered pecan nut or cherry into the top of each. Bake at 180 °C for 15 minutes. Remove to wire racks to cool.
Makes 48

Almond Crescents

Crisp and clove-scented, these Kourabiedes are the national cookies of Greece, served at weddings, birthday celebrations and christenings. Similar to shortbread in texture, they should be handled delicately.

250 g soft butter, preferably unsalted
125 ml castor sugar
1 egg yolk
15 ml brandy
650 ml cake flour
100 ml cornflour
125 ml finely chopped, toasted almonds
whole cloves
sifted icing sugar

Cream butter and sugar until pale and fluffy. Add yolk beaten with brandy and beat until combined. Sift flour with cornflour and beat in gradually. Add almonds and knead until smooth. Pinch off small pieces and shape into crescents. Place on ungreased baking trays and insert a clove into the top of each. Bake at 150 °C for 30 minutes. Test by cutting one in half – there should be no trace of a buttery streak. Carefully roll crescents, while still warm, in icing sugar. Place on wire racks and sift more icing sugar over – the crescents should be well coated. Leave until cold before storing in airtight container.
Makes 48

Coconut Cherry Winks

Bright, dainty, irresistible little melt-in-the-mouth morsels.

125 g very soft butter
50 ml sifted icing sugar
200 ml cake flour
25 ml cornflour
2 ml vanilla essence
75 ml desiccated coconut
12 glacé cherries, halved
25 ml water (optional)

Cream butter and icing sugar. Sift flour and cornflour, add to creamed mixture and beat well. Add vanilla and coconut, adding up to 25 ml water if the dough is too stiff. Combine thoroughly. Using a piping bag fitted with a star-shaped nozzle, pipe onto ungreased baking trays. Press half a cherry into each and bake at 160 °C for 20 minutes until pale gold. Cool on wire rack.
Makes 16-24, depending on size

NOTE
It is important to use soft butter, extra large eggs, and an electric beater, otherwise the mixture will not bind sufficiently.

Spiced Coffee Drops

Make a big batch of these large, disc-shaped, soft and spicy biscuits.

250 g soft butter
500 ml light brown sugar
2 eggs
15 ml instant coffee granules
125 ml cold water
4 x 250 ml white bread flour plus 10 ml extra
5 ml bicarbonate of soda
2 ml salt
5 ml ground cinnamon
2 ml grated nutmeg
large pinch ground cloves
chocolate Morsels (optional)

Cream butter and sugar. Beat in eggs, one at a time. Dissolve coffee in water and add together with the 10 ml flour. Beat well. Sift flour, bicarbonate of soda, salt and spices. Mix into creamed mixture to make a soft dough. Chill for at least 1 hour. Using a teaspoon, push mounds of dough off onto oiled baking trays, leaving room for spreading. Press a chocolate Morsel lightly into the top of each, or leave plain. Bake at 180 °C for 13-15 minutes, until golden brown. Using a spatula, remove to wire rack to cool. Store in airtight container.
Makes about 80

Muesli Bars

125 g soft butter
250 ml light brown sugar
1 egg, beaten
250 ml wholewheat flour
125 ml rolled oats
250 ml muesli
100 ml desiccated coconut
125 ml sultanas
5 ml baking powder
5 ml ground cinnamon
2 ml ground mixed spice
125 ml chopped nuts or
75 ml sunflower seeds

Cream butter and sugar. Add egg and beat well. Add flour, oats, muesli, coconut, sultanas, baking powder, spices and nuts or sunflower seeds. Mix well to a soft dough – use an electric beater. The mixture will seem rather crumbly, but it binds together as you press it out. Press out flat into a lightly oiled 33 x 20 cm Swiss roll tin, and bake at 180 °C for 20 minutes. Cut into bars – they will be very soft, but will crisp on cooling. Cool in tin, remove carefully to wire rack and leave until cold.
Makes 24

Coconut Macaroons

1 egg
125 ml castor sugar
2 ml vanilla essence
pinch salt
500 ml desiccated coconut
quartered glacé cherries or halved almonds

Beat egg, sugar, vanilla and salt until very light and creamy. Gradually beat in coconut, a little at a time, to make a moist and crumbly mixture. Using a teaspoon, push little mounds onto baking tray which has been oiled and dusted with cornflour. Pinch together into pyramids. Top with cherries or almonds. Bake at 150 °C for 20 minutes or until beginning to brown. Gently loosen with spatula and remove to wire rack to cool.
Makes 20

Chocolate Crinkles

The ultimate crunchy sandwiched biscuits, filled with melted chocolate.

125 g soft butter
125 ml castor sugar
150 ml self-raising flour
pinch salt
150 ml wholewheat flour
150 ml desiccated coconut
2 ml vanilla essence
25 ml cocoa powder
30 ml boiling water
melted dark or milk chocolate

Cream butter and sugar. Add self-raising flour sifted with salt. When well mixed add wholewheat flour, coconut and vanilla. Mix well, then stir in cocoa creamed with boiling water. Beat into flour mixture to make a soft dough. Gather into a ball and pinch off small pieces the size of large marbles. Place on oiled baking trays. Press down heavily with fork to score deeply. Bake at 180 °C for 15 minutes. Cool on wire rack, and when cold, sandwich together with melted chocolate.
Makes 22 sandwiches

Raisin Oat Bars

Soft, cake-like bars.

60 g soft butter
60 ml light brown sugar
50 ml golden syrup
2 eggs, lightly beaten
125 ml cake flour
7 ml baking powder
5 ml ground mixed spice
125 ml wholewheat flour
200 ml seedless raisins
125 ml rolled oats
icing sugar (optional)

Cream butter and sugar. Add syrup and eggs and beat well. Sift cake flour, baking powder and spice and mix into creamed mixture. Add wholewheat flour, raisins and oats. Combine well – the mixture will be soft and sticky. Turn into an oiled 21 x 21 cm baking tin. Spread evenly, using the back of a dampened spoon or rubber spatula. Bake at 180 °C for 25 minutes, until firm. Cut into bars and cool in tin. Leave plain, or, before removing, dust with icing sugar. Store in an airtight container.
Makes 18 large bars

Crisp Chocolate Crinkles and elegant Vanilla Viennese Twirls.

Fruity Oat Crisps

125 g soft butter
125 ml light brown sugar
2 ml vanilla essence
125 ml cake flour
375 ml rolled oats
200 ml fruit cake mix
pinch salt
2 ml bicarbonate of soda
10 ml hot water

Cream butter, sugar and vanilla. Add flour, oats, fruit and salt. Mix well, then beat in bicarbonate of soda dissolved in hot water. Mix to a soft dough, pinch off small pieces and roll into balls, flouring palms occasionally if necessary. Place on oiled baking trays and press down lightly with a fork. Bake at 180 °C for 15 minutes. Leave to crisp on trays for a few minutes before removing to wire rack to cool.
Makes 28

Peanut Butter Biscuits

50 ml peanut butter
125 g soft butter
2 ml vanilla essence
200 ml light brown sugar
1 egg, lightly beaten
250 ml white bread flour
plus 5 ml extra
pinch salt
2 ml bicarbonate of soda
250 ml brown bread flour

Cream peanut butter, butter and vanilla. Beat in sugar very well or it will not dissolve. Add egg plus the 5 ml extra flour and beat well. Mix in white bread flour sifted with salt and bicarbonate of soda. Finally mix in brown bread flour and knead until dough holds together. Roll small pieces into balls and place on oiled baking trays, leaving room to spread. Flatten with a wet fork, in a criss-cross pattern, and bake at 180 °C for 20 minutes. Cool on a wire rack.
Makes 36

Spiced Coconut Biscuits

A simple, crunchy cookie with spices adding a lovely zip to the flavour.

125 g soft butter
200 ml castor sugar
1 egg
2 ml vanilla essence
500 ml self-raising flour
pinch salt
5 ml ground cinnamon
1 ml grated nutmeg
200 ml desiccated coconut
pecan nuts, halved (optional)

Cream butter and sugar until light. Beat egg with vanilla and add, mixing well. Sift flour, salt and spices and add, then finally mix in coconut and combine thoroughly. Knead into a ball with your hands, then pinch off small pieces and roll into balls. Place on oiled baking trays, allowing for spreading, and press flat with a fork, or press half a pecan nut into the top of each. Bake at 180 °C for 15-18 minutes until a deep beige colour. Cool on wire rack.
Makes 36

Crunchies

A super version of this old favourite; it is designed to fill the average 37 x 25 cm baking tray to the brim, requires slightly less butter and sugar than usual, and is made extra nutritious with the addition of raisins and/or sunflower seeds.

750 ml rolled oats
375 ml light brown sugar
250 ml brown bread flour
125 ml cake flour
300 ml desiccated coconut
125 ml seedless raisins
125 ml sunflower seeds
250 g butter
50 ml honey
10 ml bicarbonate of soda

Mix oats, sugar, flours, coconut, raisins and sunflower seeds. Melt butter and honey over low heat – the mixture will brown slowly and this adds to the flavour. Stir in bicarbonate of soda. When mixture froths, add to dry ingredients, mix well and press firmly into an oiled 37 x 25 cm baking tray. Bake on middle shelf of oven at 180 °C for 18-20 minutes until richly browned. Cut into jumbo bars and remove when cold.
Makes 30 jumbo bars

Chocolate Logs

250 g soft butter
125 ml sifted icing sugar
5 ml vanilla essence
15 ml cocoa powder
400 ml cake flour
100 ml cornflour
pinch salt

VANILLA BUTTER ICING
125 ml sifted icing sugar
a nut of soft butter
1 ml vanilla essence
5 ml milk
chocolate vermicelli

Cream butter, icing sugar and vanilla until light. Sift cocoa, flour, cornflour and salt and add to creamed mixture. Mix to a soft dough and fill piping bag fitted with a fluted nozzle. Pipe 7 cm-long logs onto ungreased baking trays. Bake at 160 °C for 30 minutes, then cool on wire rack.

To make icing, combine all ingredients, except vermicelli, until creamy. Spread over tops of logs and sprinkle with vermicelli.
Makes 36

NOTE
- *If preferred, the icing may be omitted, in which case simply brush the unbaked logs with lightly beaten egg white, sprinkle with chocolate vermicelli and bake as above.*

Vanilla Viennese Twirls

Melt-in-the-mouth little shortbreads, sandwiched with vanilla butter icing.

250 g soft butter
100 ml sifted icing sugar
500 ml cake flour
50 ml cornflour
5 ml vanilla essence

ICING
125 ml sifted icing sugar
25 ml soft butter
few drops vanilla essence

Cream butter and sugar. Sift flour and cornflour. Add to creamed mixture together with vanilla and mix well to a soft dough. Pipe rosettes onto ungreased baking trays and bake at 160 °C for 20 minutes until pale gold. Cool on wire rack.

Beat ingredients for icing together until smooth. Use to sandwich biscuits.
Makes 24 single biscuits

Chocolate Chip Biscuits

Large, crisp cookies studded with nuts and chocolate Morsels which, unlike grated chocolate, will not melt in the baking, but retain their shape.

125 g soft butter
100 ml castor sugar
60 ml light brown sugar
1 egg
2 ml vanilla essence
300 ml cake flour
50 ml cornflour
2 ml bicarbonate of soda
pinch salt
125 ml chopped walnuts or pecan nuts
200 ml chocolate Morsels

Cream butter with both sugars. Beat egg with vanilla and add, mixing well. Sift flour, cornflour, bicarbonate of soda and salt. Add to creamed mixture, mixing to a soft dough. Stir in nuts and chocolate Morsels. Shape dough into a ball, pinch off pieces and roll into balls, flouring your palms occasionally if necessary. Place on oiled baking trays, leaving room for spreading, and flatten lightly with a fork. Bake at 180 °C for 15 minutes. Cool on wire rack.
Makes 40

Fruit Oat Squares

These biscuits keep well and are similar to crunchies, except that they're softer and bursting with fruit and other wholesome ingredients.

250 g fruit cake mix (scant 500 ml)
250 g butter
30 ml honey
625 ml rolled oats
250 ml wholewheat flour
250 ml white bread flour
100 ml wheat germ
250 ml desiccated coconut
200 ml light brown sugar
10 ml ground mixed spice
10 ml bicarbonate of soda

Put fruit, butter and honey into heavy saucepan and bring to a slow boil, stirring to melt the butter. Mix oats, flours, wheat germ, coconut, sugar and spice in large bowl. Add bicarbonate of soda to hot mixture, stirring vigorously, and when mixture froths stir into dry ingredients. Mix very well and then press into an oiled 37 x 25 cm baking tray. Pat in firmly and evenly, and bake on middle shelf of oven at 180 °C for 15-20 minutes until browned. Cut into squares and leave in tin until cold.
Makes 35

NOTE
● *As with most of my biscuit mixtures, it is important to use soft butter, extra large eggs, and an electric beater, otherwise the butter might not 'melt' sufficiently to bind the mixture.*

Lemon Sultana Snaps

These super biscuits spread into very crisp, golden-brown rounds.

125 g soft butter
2 ml vanilla essence
finely grated rind of 1 lemon
125 ml sugar
125 ml cake flour
pinch salt
2 ml bicarbonate of soda
125 ml wholewheat flour
125 ml bleached sultanas

Cream butter with vanilla, lemon rind and sugar until light. Sift cake flour with salt and bicarbonate of soda, add to creamed mixture and mix. Add wholewheat flour and when combined, add sultanas. Mix well then knead into a ball. Pinch off small pieces, roll into balls, and place on oiled baking trays, leaving room for spreading. Flatten two ways, making a criss-cross pattern, with a fork dipped into water. Bake at 180 °C for 15 minutes. Leave to crisp on tray for a minute before removing with a spatula to wire rack to cool.
Makes 28

Wholewheat and Oat Ginger Crisps

Thin, crunchy, economical cookies.

250 g soft butter
250 ml light brown sugar
250 ml wholewheat flour
750 ml rolled oats
15 ml ground ginger
2 ml salt
2 ml vanilla essence
2 ml bicarbonate of soda
50 ml boiling water

Cream butter and sugar until light. Add flour, oats, ginger, salt and vanilla. Mix well. Add bicarbonate of soda dissolved in boiling water. Combine thoroughly and then work into a soft ball. Scoop off teaspoonfuls of dough, and push off onto oiled baking tray, leaving room for spreading. Bake at 180 °C for about 15 minutes until lightly browned and spread into flat rounds. Leave on tray for a minute to crisp before removing with spatula to wire rack to cool.
Makes 48

Orange Cookie Press Biscuits

Delicately flavoured, with a short texture – serve prettily shaped and plain, or sandwich with orange-flavoured butter icing.

125 g soft butter
50 ml castor sugar
finely grated rind of half an orange
250 ml cake flour
50 ml cornflour
125 ml desiccated coconut

Cream butter, sugar and rind until very light. Mix in flour sifted with cornflour. Add coconut and then beat well until mixture forms a ball. Using a cookie press, press into desired shapes onto ungreased baking trays. Bake at 160 °C for 20 minutes. Cool on wire rack.
Makes 24

FROM THE TOP: *Fruit Oat Squares; Lemon Sultana Snaps; Orange Cookie Press Biscuits; Chocolate Chip Biscuits.*

Simple Cocoa Crisps; Orange Van der Hum Wafers; Quick Date and Nut Bars.

Simple Cocoa Crisps

Economical and very quick to make.

125 ml light brown sugar
125 ml white sugar
125 ml oil
1 egg, beaten
125 ml desiccated coconut
2 ml vanilla essence
pinch salt
2 ml bicarbonate of soda
125 ml brown bread flour
500 ml rolled oats
25 ml cocoa powder

Put ingredients into bowl in above order and beat until well mixed – the mixture will be crumbly. Press together into a ball, then scoop up teaspoonfuls and place on oiled baking trays, leaving plenty of room for spreading. Pinch into little pyramids with your fingers. Bake at 180 °C for 20 minutes. Leave on trays to crisp for 1 minute before removing with spatula to wire rack to cool.
Makes 28

Walnut Fridge Crisps

Delicious, crisp cookies.

500 ml cake flour
5 ml baking powder
1 ml salt
2 ml bicarbonate of soda
5 ml ground mixed spice
125 g butter
125 ml light brown sugar
125 ml sugar
1 egg
5 ml vanilla essence
125 ml finely chopped walnuts

Sift flour, baking powder, salt, bicarbonate of soda and mixed spice. Cream butter and slowly add brown and white sugar, beating well. Beat egg with vanilla and add to butter mixture, then mix in the flour mixture – an electric beater is perfect for the job. Lastly add walnuts. Form into 2 long sausages, wrap in greaseproof paper and chill until firm enough to slice. Cut into thin rounds and bake on an ungreased baking tray at 180 °C for about 15 minutes. Cool on wire rack. Store in an airtight container with sugar between the layers.
Makes about 54

Oat, Sultana and Coconut Bars

Quick-mix, crunchy bars.

60 g butter
60 ml oil
250 ml rolled oats
125 ml sultanas
250 ml self-raising flour
125 ml sugar
125 ml desiccated coconut
2 ml vanilla essence

Place butter and oil in a small saucepan and heat gently just until butter melts. Mix remaining ingredients and stir in melted shortening. Using an electric beater, mix well to a soft, crumbly consistency. Press dough firmly into an oiled 21 x 21 cm baking tin. Bake on middle shelf of oven at 180 °C for 25 minutes, until just beginning to colour. Cut into bars and leave in tin until cold.
Makes 18

Carrot, Date and Sunflower Seed Biscuits

Big, flat, quick-mix cookies.

125 ml light brown sugar
125 ml white sugar
125 g soft butter
1 egg, beaten
250 ml coarsely grated carrot
5 ml ground cinnamon
1 ml grated nutmeg
pinch salt
2 ml bicarbonate of soda
125 ml brown bread flour
500 ml rolled oats
125 g dates, finely chopped
125 ml sunflower seeds, preferably toasted

Beat all ingredients, except sunflower seeds, until very well combined. Add sunflower seeds and mix to a soft dough. Scoop up teaspoonfuls and push off onto oiled baking trays, leaving plenty of room for spreading. Bake at 180 °C for 15 minutes, then allow to crisp on trays for about 1 minute before carefully removing, using a spatula, to wire rack to cool.
Makes 40

Chinese Chews

These soft bars, rather like a light fruit cake, firms up with storing and develop a delicious, gingery flavour.

125 g soft butter
200 ml light brown sugar
2 eggs
250 ml white bread flour
5 ml baking powder
125 ml chopped walnuts or pecan nuts
125 g pitted dates, chopped
100 ml chopped glacé cherries
2 large knobs preserved ginger, chopped
2 ml vanilla essence
castor sugar

Cream butter and sugar. Add eggs one by one, beating well. Sift flour and baking powder, add nuts and fruit and toss to mix. Stir into creamed mixture, add vanilla and mix well to a thick batter. Turn into an oiled 26 x 21 cm baking tin, spreading evenly, and bake at 180 °C for 25 minutes or until light brown and firm. Dust with castor sugar, cut into bars and leave in tin until cold.
Makes 24

Orange Van der Hum Wafers

Light, melt-in-the-mouth little slices, to serve with sorbets or ice cream.

125 g soft butter
125 ml castor sugar
25 ml Van der Hum liqueur
250 ml cake flour
50 ml cornflour
pinch salt
5 ml finely grated orange rind
extra castor sugar

Cream butter, sugar and liqueur until fluffy. Sift flour, cornflour and salt and blend into butter mixture. Mix in orange rind and shape into a ball, then roll into a long, smooth sausage. Wrap in greaseproof paper and chill for about 1 hour. Slice thinly, using a sharp knife, and arrange on an ungreased baking tray, leaving room for spreading. Bake at 180 °C for 10 minutes, or until pale gold. Dust with castor sugar, cool slightly on baking tray, then lift carefully onto wire racks to cool completely. Store in airtight container.
Makes 42-48

Quick Date and Nut Bars

250 g pitted dates, chopped
2 eggs, lightly beaten
100 ml light brown sugar
60 ml oil
125 ml wholewheat flour
125 ml rolled oats
5 ml baking powder
5 ml ground mixed spice
1 ml salt
125 ml chopped walnuts or pecan nuts
2 ml vanilla essence
icing sugar

Mix all ingredients, except icing sugar, in the order given. Spoon evenly into an oiled 21 x 21 cm baking tin and bake at 180 °C for 25 minutes, until brown and firm. Cut into bars and cool in tin. Dust with icing sugar when cold.
Makes 18 large bars

Muesli Munchies

125 ml cake flour
5 ml cream of tartar
2 ml bicarbonate of soda
pinch salt
5 ml ground mixed spice
250 ml wholewheat flour
200 ml light brown sugar
150 ml oil
2 eggs
200 ml muesli
100 ml sultanas
125 ml desiccated coconut

Sift together cake flour, cream of tartar, bicarbonate of soda, salt and spice. Add wholewheat flour. Whisk together sugar, oil and eggs. Add to dry ingredients together with muesli, sultanas and coconut. Mix very well to a soft dough. Push large teaspoonfuls off onto oiled baking trays, leaving plenty of room for spreading. Flatten lightly with tines of a fork dipped into water. Bake at 180 °C for 18 minutes. Using a spatula, transfer to wire racks to cool.
Makes 30

Brown Honey and Sunflower Cookies

250 ml rolled oats
250 ml white bread flour
125 ml sugar
125 ml desiccated coconut
125 ml currants, plumped in hot water
125 ml sunflower seeds, preferably toasted
60 g butter
60 ml oil
30 ml honey
2 ml bicarbonate of soda
15 ml hot water
1 egg, beaten
2 ml vanilla essence

Mix oats, flour, sugar, coconut, drained currants, and sunflower seeds. Heat butter, oil and honey until just melted. Dissolve bicarbonate of soda in hot water and add to melted mixture. Stir foaming mixture into dry ingredients. Mix well to a crumbly dough – using an electric beater – then add egg and vanilla and continue beating until mixture forms a soft ball. Push teaspoonfuls of mixture off onto lightly oiled baking trays, leaving room for spreading, and bake on middle shelf of oven at 180 °C for 15 minutes or until browned and firm. Cool on wire racks.
Makes 28

Orange and Oat Macaroons

This recipe makes a big batch.

250 ml light brown sugar
250 ml white sugar
250 ml oil
2 eggs, beaten
250 ml desiccated coconut
5 ml vanilla essence
2 ml salt
5 ml bicarbonate of soda
10 ml finely grated orange rind
100 ml chopped mixed peel
250 ml white bread flour
4 x 250 ml rolled oats

Place ingredients in a large bowl in the order given. Mix well, then shape into a soft ball. The dough will be loose and slippery. Place teaspoonfuls on oiled baking trays, pinching gently to shape and leaving plenty of room for spreading. Bake at 180 °C for 15 minutes. Leave to crisp on trays for a minute. Using a spatula, remove to wire rack to cool. Store in airtight container, with sugar sprinkled between each layer.
Makes 80

Spiced Mincemeat Bars

BASE
4 x 250 ml cake flour
15 ml baking powder
2 ml salt
10 ml ground cinnamon
5 ml ground mixed spice
400 ml icing sugar
250 g soft butter
2 eggs, beaten

FILLING
1 x 454 g jar fruit mincemeat
1 large Granny Smith apple, peeled and coarsely grated
25 ml brandy
extra icing sugar

Sift flour, baking powder, salt, spices and icing sugar. Rub in the butter, and then add eggs. (An electric mixer may be used.) Knead to a ball, wrap and freeze until hard, about 45 minutes. Remove three-quarters of the dough from the freezer and grate coarsely into a large, lightly oiled square or rectangular baking tin. Pat down with hands to form a smooth, 5 mm-thick base.

For the filling, mix mincemeat, apple and brandy, and spread evenly over dough. Remove remaining dough from freezer and grate coarsely over the top, spreading evenly with a fork. Bake at 160 °C for 50 minutes or until crisp. Cut into bars and cool in tin. Dust with icing sugar, then remove and place on wire rack until completely cold.
Makes 40

Honeyed Seed Cookies

Intriguing, caramel-coloured biscuits, containing sunflower seeds and wholewheat flour. The crisp sesame topping makes them singularly attractive cookies.

125 g soft butter
2 ml vanilla essence
125 ml light brown sugar
25 ml honey
150 ml cake flour
pinch salt
2 ml bicarbonate of soda
150 ml wholewheat flour
100 ml sunflower seeds, preferably lightly toasted
about 40 ml sesame seeds

Cream butter, vanilla, sugar and honey. Sift cake flour with salt and bicarbonate of soda, and mix in. Add wholewheat flour and sunflower seeds. Beat well to make a soft dough, then shape into a ball. Pinch off small pieces and flatten between palms. Dip tops in sesame seeds, coating thoroughly. Place on oiled baking trays, allowing room for spreading. Bake at 180 °C for about 12 minutes, until browned. Allow to crisp on trays for 1 minute before removing to wire rack to cool.
Makes 26

Orange, Honey and Raisin Crisps

Nutritious brown biscuits made with oil, honey and wholewheat flour.

125 ml oil
25 ml honey
125 ml sugar
5 ml finely grated orange rind
200 ml wholewheat flour
100 ml self-raising flour
pinch salt
125 ml desiccated coconut
75 ml seedless raisins
1 egg, lightly beaten

Whisk together the oil, honey, sugar and rind. Add flours, salt, coconut and raisins. Mix well, add egg and mix to a soft, rather oily dough. Roll into balls and place on lightly oiled baking trays. Flatten with bottom of a glass. Bake at 180 °C for 15 minutes or until firm and richly browned. Cool on wire rack.
Makes 28

CHOCOLATE DIGESTIVES

These crisp, sweet and wholesome biscuits may be served plain or topped with chocolate.

750 ml rolled oats
250 ml wholewheat flour
125 ml self-raising flour
1 ml salt
60 ml castor sugar
125 g butter
50 ml honey
40-50 ml milk

TOPPING
100 g dark chocolate
10 ml water
10 ml butter

Put oats into processor fitted with grinding blade and process until fairly fine, but do not grind to a meal. Mix with both flours and salt. Add sugar. Melt butter with honey over low heat – the mixture must just have melted without bubbling. Slowly beat into flour mixture. Mix well and then add just enough milk to make a soft dough. Pat out onto lightly floured board and then roll flat, about 3 mm thick, with a rolling pin. Using a 6 cm cutter, cut into rounds, place on oiled baking trays and prick each biscuit well with a fork. Bake at 180 °C for 12 minutes – watch carefully, as they brown quickly round the edges. Cool on wire rack.

Make topping by breaking up chocolate and melting over low heat with water and butter. Remove and stir until smooth, then spread thinly over top of each cooled biscuit. Return to rack to set before storing.
Makes 50

FROM THE TOP: *Chocolate Digestives; Spiced Mincemeat Bars; Orange and Oat Macaroons; Honeyed Seed Cookies.*

Caramel Squares; Featherlight Chocolate Swirls; Iced Chocolate Squares; Clove-studded Spicy Brown Biscuits.

Caramel Squares

Rather like fudge – and the richest, sweetest biscuits in the book.

250 g butter
200 ml sugar
500 ml cake flour
5 ml baking powder
5 ml ground cinnamon
50-75 ml finely chopped pecan nuts

FILLING
1 x 225 g can condensed milk
25 ml golden syrup
25 ml sugar
25 ml water
25 ml butter
2 ml vanilla essence

Cream butter and sugar. Sift flour with baking powder and cinnamon and add to creamed mixture. Mix well – the dough will be very soft. Press two-thirds of the mixture evenly into a lightly oiled, 33 x 20 cm Swiss roll tin. Add the nuts to the remaining third, wrap in greaseproof paper and place in freezer. Bake the base at 160 °C for 15 minutes.

Meanwhile, make filling by placing condensed milk, syrup, sugar, water and butter in small, heavy-based saucepan. Bring to the boil over low heat, stirring all the time to dissolve the sugar, and then boil gently until thick and a light caramel in colour. Stir continually and watch carefully that it doesn't catch on the bottom as it burns very easily. Remove from the heat and add vanilla, then pour over half-baked base, spreading evenly. Grate chilled dough coarsely over the top. Bake on the middle shelf of the oven at 160 °C for 25 minutes or until the filling is the colour of fudge. Cut into squares and leave to cool in the tin before removing.

Makes 24

HINT
- *When measuring honey or syrup, use a measure which has been oiled, or used to measure oil – the honey or syrup will slide out easily.*

Featherlight Chocolate Swirls

A very light and fluffy mixture, resulting in pale, chocolaty, melt-in-the-mouth dainties.

125 g soft butter
125 ml castor sugar
1 egg, lightly beaten
2 ml vanilla essence
400 ml self-raising flour
100 ml cornflour
50 g dark chocolate
50 ml water
glacé cherries

Cream butter and sugar until light. Beat in egg and vanilla. Sift flour with cornflour and mix in. Place broken up chocolate in small container, add water, and melt over simmering water. Add to creamed mixture and beat until thoroughly combined. Use an electric beater, and the mixture will soon become the correct consistency for piping. Fill piping bag fitted with a star nozzle and pipe in small whorls onto baking trays lined with waxed paper, leaving room for spreading. Press a quartered cherry into the top of each. Bake at 160 °C for 20 minutes. Using a spatula, remove to wire rack to cool.

Makes 24-30

Clove-Studded Spicy Brown Biscuits

These easy-to-make, economical cookies should be kept for a few days to allow the flavour to develop.

125 g soft butter
200 ml sugar
1 egg, beaten
50 ml golden syrup
750 ml white bread flour
5 ml bicarbonate of soda
2 ml salt
5 ml ground cinnamon
10 ml ground mixed spice
whole cloves

Cream butter, sugar, egg and syrup. Sift dry ingredients together and add. Mix into a ball, pinch off pieces, roll into small balls and place on oiled baking trays. Press a clove into the centre of each and bake on middle shelf of oven at 180 °C for 12 minutes, or until lightly browned. Cool on wire rack.

Makes 40

Iced Chocolate Squares

A crunchie base spread with a dark, sweet topping.

BASE
125 ml sugar
250 ml brown bread flour
250 ml desiccated coconut
25 ml cocoa powder
2 ml bicarbonate of soda
250 ml rolled oats
125 g soft butter
2 ml vanilla essence

TOPPING
350 ml sifted icing sugar
10 ml cocoa powder
small nut of butter
few drops vanilla essence
hot water

In a large bowl mix sugar, flour, coconut, cocoa, bicarbonate of soda and oats. Beat in butter and vanilla until thoroughly combined. Press mixture firmly into an oiled 33 x 20 cm Swiss roll tin and bake at 180 °C for 20 minutes. Cut into squares and leave in tin to cool slightly before spreading with topping.

For the topping, beat icing sugar, cocoa, butter and vanilla together, adding just enough hot water to make a spreading consistency – do not use too much or the icing will not set. Spread over base and re-cut squares when set. Remove when cold.

Makes 30 large squares

Fruit Drops

These are economical, spicy and wholesome chews, using oil, dried fruit and wholewheat flour.

250 ml cake flour
2 ml baking powder
5 ml bicarbonate of soda
1 ml salt
5 ml ground cinnamon
2 ml grated nutmeg
pinch ground cloves
2 eggs
150 ml oil
125 ml sugar
125 ml light brown sugar
250 ml wholewheat flour
250 ml rolled oats
125 ml desiccated coconut
500 ml fruit cake mix

Sift together cake flour, baking powder, bicarbonate of soda, salt and spices. Beat eggs well with oil and both sugars. Mix into sifted mixture, then add wholewheat flour, oats, coconut and fruit. Mix well and then push teaspoonfuls off onto well-oiled baking trays, leaving room for spreading. Bake in the centre of the oven at 180 °C for 12-15 minutes until browned. Cool on wire rack.
Makes 48

Five-Star Fruit Squares

Richly browned, sweet, cake-like bars.

500 ml self-raising flour
5 ml ground cinnamon
2 ml grated nutmeg
pinch ground cloves
250 ml sugar
250 ml desiccated coconut
375 ml fruit cake mix
100 ml toasted sunflower seeds
200 ml oil
100 g butter, melted
2 eggs, beaten
250 ml All-Bran flakes, coarsely crushed
5 ml vanilla essence

Sift flour with spices into a large mixing bowl. Using a wooden spoon, mix in remaining ingredients, stirring well to combine. Press mixture very firmly and evenly into an oiled 26 x 20 x 6 cm baking tin or small roaster, rather like crunchies. Bake on middle shelf of oven at 180 °C for 35 minutes until risen, browned and firm – do not overbake. Cut into bars or squares and leave in tin until cold.
Makes 24-30

NOTE
- *If preferred, 250 ml oil may be used and the butter omitted – the texture will be less moist, rather like a biscuit.*

Date, Nut and Oat Biscuits

125 g butter
125 ml sugar
1 egg, beaten
125 g pitted dates, chopped
125 ml chopped walnuts or pecan nuts
250 ml cake flour or brown bread flour
2 ml baking powder
2 ml bicarbonate of soda
pinch salt
250 ml rolled oats
125 ml desiccated coconut
2 ml vanilla essence

Melt butter, add sugar and mix well. Pour into mixing bowl and add egg. Stir in dates together with walnuts or pecan nuts. Sift flour, baking powder, bicarbonate of soda and salt and add to butter mixture, tipping in any bran left in sifter. Add oats, coconut and vanilla. Mix well – the mixture will be soft, but firms up on cooling. Shape into small balls and place on lightly oiled baking trays, leaving room for spreading. Flatten lightly with a fork and bake at 180 °C for 12 minutes or until golden brown. Cool on wire rack.
Makes about 30

Almond Meringue Fingers

2 egg whites
250 ml castor sugar
125 ml finely chopped almonds
dark chocolate (optional)

Whisk egg whites until fairly stiff. Whisk in sugar, a little at a time, and beat until mixture is stiff and glossy. Fold in almonds. Fill piping bag with mixture and, using a plain nozzle, pipe 8 cm-long fingers onto baking trays which have been oiled and dusted with cornflour. Bake at 140 °C for 1½ hours, until pale beige in colour, then switch off oven and leave until cold before opening the door. If using the chocolate finish, melt dark chocolate with 5-10 ml water and dip in the end of each meringue finger, turning to coat. Place on wire rack to set.
Makes 20

Oat and Coconut Biscuits

Large, crunchy biscuits.

250 g soft butter
250 ml light brown sugar
250 ml brown bread flour
500 ml rolled oats
250 ml desiccated coconut
2 ml salt
5 ml vanilla essence
2 ml bicarbonate of soda
50 ml hot water

Cream butter and sugar very well. Add flour, oats, coconut, salt and vanilla. Dissolve bicarbonate of soda in the hot water and add. Mix well. Roll into small balls, or push from a teaspoon into rough heaps on oiled baking trays, leaving plenty of room for spreading. Flatten lightly with a fork and bake at 180 °C for 15 minutes or until pale brown. Remove carefully, using a spatula, and leave on wire racks to crisp.
Makes 36

Quick Fruit Bars

Dark and fruity, nutty and chewy, this recipe makes a big batch of lunch-box specials.

500 ml self-raising flour
375 ml light brown sugar
375 ml desiccated coconut
250 g fruit cake mix (scant 500 ml)
125 ml chopped pecan nuts or chopped, toasted almonds
2 eggs
5 ml vanilla essence
125 g butter
100 ml oil
15 ml cocoa powder
10 ml ground mixed spice

In a large bowl mix flour, sugar, coconut, fruit and nuts. Stir in eggs beaten with vanilla. Melt together the butter, oil, cocoa and mixed spice over low heat. Add to flour/fruit mixture and mix well. Press firmly into an oiled 26 x 21 cm baking tin (the batter will be rather moist and slippery, but this is correct) and bake at 180 °C for 40 minutes until firm. Cut into 24 jumbo bars or into 36 medium squares and leave to cool in tin.
Makes 24-36

Lemon Sesame Snaps (page 9); Almond Meringue Fingers; Fruit Drops.

Chocolate Oat Fridge Squares

No oven required. Once mixed and sliced, store these squares in the fridge.

250 ml sugar
75 ml cocoa powder
125 ml milk
125 g butter
200 ml seedless raisins
pinch salt
750 ml rolled oats
250 ml desiccated coconut
5 ml vanilla essence

Put sugar, cocoa, milk, butter, raisins and salt into heavy-based saucepan. Bring to the boil over low heat, stirring all the time and watching that the mixture does not catch. Simmer for 5 minutes, then remove from stove and stir in oats, coconut and vanilla. Mix very well and then spoon into shallow, buttered dish, patting mixture in to a thickness of about 2,5 cm. Cool, then cut into 28 squares, using a knife dipped into water. Keep refrigerated.
Makes 28

NOTE

- *When melting chocolate be careful not to overheat it, and do not stir. If too thick for easy dipping, it may be thinned down with just a dash of boiling water and then stirred until smooth.*

Gingerbread Men

Gingerbread 'people' are traditional party fare and may be simply decorated with currants for eyes, and buttons down the middle of the body, or more elaborately iced after baking, using a very thin nozzle to pipe on hair, mouths, bow ties, collars, even shoes and aprons. If decorating before baking, it is important to brush the biscuit with unbeaten egg white, not only to secure the currants, but to provide a shiny finish, and if you do not have a gingerbread cutter, simply use animal shapes or any other decorative cutters.

125 g soft butter
125 ml light brown sugar
30 ml golden syrup
1 egg, lightly beaten
600 ml cake flour
5 ml bicarbonate of soda
15 ml ground ginger

SPECIAL DECORATIVE ICING
400-500 ml icing sugar
50 ml egg white (about 1 large egg)
6 drops lemon juice

Cream butter, sugar and syrup until light and fluffy. Beat in egg. Sift flour, bicarbonate of soda and ginger. Beat into creamed mixture, and when well mixed, knead lightly. Using a floured rolling pin, roll out on lightly floured board and cut into shapes. Arrange on oiled baking trays, apply egg white and currants and bake on middle shelf of oven at 180 °C for 10 minutes. Allow to cool slightly on the trays before removing to wire racks.

For the icing, sift icing sugar. Using a fork, beat egg white until foamy. Slowly beat in icing sugar, using a wooden spoon and beating well between additions. When a thick, piping consistency has been reached, beat in lemon juice. Pipe onto cooled gingerbread shapes as suggested, and leave on wire rack to cool and set.

Brighten a party with Gingerbread Men, Party Faces, gingerbread teddies and colourful meringue nests.

MERINGUES

Perfect meringues, pale and crisp, are not difficult to make and the following foolproof recipe may be used in a variety of different ways, with imaginative shapes and decorations making them ideal for children's parties. To ensure success, follow the instructions carefully.

4 egg whites at room temperature
12 drops lemon juice
250 ml castor sugar
10 ml cornflour

The mixing bowl (preferably not plastic) and beaters must be spotlessly clean and free from grease. Whisk egg white with lemon juice to soft peak stage. While beating, add 150 ml of the sugar, a little at a time and beat until very stiff. Using a metal spoon fold in remaining 100 ml sugar and cornflour. (The addition of cornflour helps in preventing weeping.) The mixture may now be spooned into a piping bag, or simply dropped in mounds, with a little peak to the tops, onto *ungreased* baking trays. (Simply line with ordinary greaseproof paper or waxed kitchen paper – the cooked meringues will peel off very easily.) Bake meringues on the middle shelf of the oven at 120 °C for 1 hour – do not open the door at all. Switch off and leave until absolutely cold before removing and storing in an airtight tin.
Makes 24 small shapes

VARIATIONS
Party Meringues
If using a piping bag, try one or more of the following ideas (none of which requires artificial food colouring) for children's parties.

- Using a plain nozzle, pipe out the letters of the alphabet.
- Pipe into circles and sprinkle with chocolate vermicelli before baking, or pipe into logs, and dip one end of each baked log into melted chocolate when cold.
- Pipe into nests, and use as containers for small sweets.
- Using a fluted nozzle, pipe into 'caterpillars' with peaked tails. For the feelers, insert two small pieces of spaghetti and dust the body lightly with a little cocoa powder.
- For meringue mice, use a plain nozzle and pipe mixture into mounds, tapering front and back. Push two tiny segments of glacé cherry into the front, for the eyes, and two short lengths of spaghetti on either side for the whiskers. Use flaked almonds for the ears, and either spaghetti or a short strip of liquorice for the tail. (Some children are allergic to liquorice, therefore spaghetti is perhaps the better choice.)

Chocolate Meringues
Use 5 ml cocoa powder for each egg white used, adding it to the sugar.

PARTY FACES

Cheerful cookies to brighten a birthday tea. Made from a basic dough, rolled and cut with a large round cutter, they may be decorated before baking, or left plain, then iced and decorated when cold. Use the suggestions below, or have fun fashioning your own funny faces. Artificially coloured icing is not necessary – the sweets and cherries are colourful enough and look best on plain white icing.

4 x 250 ml cake flour
5 ml baking powder
2 ml salt
250 ml castor sugar
250 g butter
2 eggs
5 ml vanilla essence

ICING
375 ml icing sugar, sifted
20 ml butter
20 ml boiling water

Sift flour, baking powder, salt and sugar. Rub in butter until finely crumbled. Beat eggs with vanilla and add. Mix well, then knead to a dough. Pat out on lightly floured board and then roll out fairly thinly, using a floured rolling pin. Cut into rounds with a 7-8 cm cutter and place on oiled baking trays, leaving room for spreading. Re-roll and cut the trimmings. If desired, decorate biscuits before baking by brushing with unbeaten egg white and lightly pressing in segments of glacé cherries for the eyes, a currant or chocolate chip for the nose, and an almond strip for the mouth. Bake on middle shelf of oven at 180 °C for 12 minutes, until pale gold and just beginning to colour round the edges. Remove to wire rack to cool.

For the icing, combine all ingredients until smooth. Coat top of each baked biscuit smoothly, using a knife dipped into boiling water. Use Smarties or chocolate chips for eyes or noses, currants for eyes, liquorice or almond strips for eyebrows and mouths, chocolate vermicelli for hair.
Makes 40

Ginger-glazed Shortbread

Delicious, gingery wedges, thinly covered with a fudgy glaze.

BASE
125 g soft butter
60 ml castor sugar
375 ml cake flour
5 ml baking powder
10 ml ground ginger

GLAZE
60 ml sifted icing sugar
25 ml butter
2 ml ground ginger
15 ml preserved ginger syrup

Cream butter and sugar until light. Sift dry ingredients and add. Mix well and then knead until mixture forms a ball. Pat out and press evenly into an ungreased, 22 cm-diameter, loose-bottomed cake tin. Prick well, press round the edge with the tines of a fork and mark into 12 wedges. Bake on middle shelf of oven at 160 °C for 40 minutes.

Just before the end of the baking time prepare glaze by combining ingredients in a small saucepan. Heat very gently until just melted – on no account allow mixture to boil. Using the back of a spoon, spread hot mixture over hot, cooked base to within 25 mm of the edge so that crimping remains visible. Cut through the wedges and leave until completely cold. Cut again, push up base and remove. Decorate with slivers of preserved ginger if desired.
Makes 12 wedges

Coconut Shortbread Fingers

Shortbread with a slight twist to the flavour.

300 ml cake flour
60 ml castor sugar
200 ml desiccated coconut
125 g soft butter, diced
extra castor sugar

Mix dry ingredients. Rub in butter thoroughly, using an electric beater, until mixture has a fine, crumbly consistency, then knead very well until dough clings together and forms a smooth ball. Press evenly into an ungreased, 21 cm square baking tin, mark into 21 fingers, and prick well. Bake on middle shelf of oven at 150 °C for 50-60 minutes. Cut through fingers, sprinkle with extra castor sugar and leave in tin until cold.
Makes 21

Rich Scots Shortbread

This is an extravagant, special-occasion shortbread. In most of the recipes, I have used a slightly more modest proportion of butter to flour; nevertheless, the results are still crisp and short. The traditional ingredients and method result in this picture-book, perfect shortbread. To shape, use decorative shortbread moulds if you have them. Dust them with cornflour each time before pressing in the dough, and it will unmould easily. Alternatively, use a layer cake tin, as follows.

125 g soft butter
50 ml castor sugar
275 ml cake flour
25 ml rice flour

Cream butter. Slowly beat in the sugar. When well mixed, gradually add flour sifted with rice flour. When thoroughly combined, knead gently until mixture holds together and forms a ball. Dust an 18 cm-diameter layer cake tin with cornflour. Shake out excess, then pat the shortbread dough in firmly and evenly. Turn out onto ungreased baking tray by running a knife round the edges, turning tin upside down, and giving it a hard shake. The shortbread 'cake' should drop out easily. If there is any cornflour on the top, use a pastry brush to remove. Crimp edges with forefinger and thumb, prick well, and score lightly into 8 wedges. Bake on middle shelf of oven at 150 °C for 45 minutes until palest beige in colour. Dust with a little extra castor sugar, cut through the wedges, and leave until cold before removing.
Makes 8 wedges

Shortbread Pennies

If you don't have a wooden stamp, preferably with a thistle design, or a shortbread mould, simply prick each round twice with the tines of a fork, to resemble buttons, in which case they are called Shortbread Buttons.

300 ml cake flour
25 ml cornflour
100 ml icing sugar
125 g soft butter
2 ml vanilla essence
castor sugar

Sift flour, cornflour and icing sugar. Rub in butter until mixture is very finely crumbled. Add vanilla and knead well to a smooth dough. This takes several minutes. Pat out on unfloured board and then roll lightly with a rolling pin to flatten evenly, 5 mm thick. Cut into rounds, using a 4 or 5 cm cutter. It is important that the rounds be of uniform thickness. Gather up off-cuts, knead, pat out and cut until all the dough has been used. Place rounds on ungreased baking tray and either stamp or prick as suggested. Bake at 150 °C for about 30 minutes until deep gold in colour. Do not allow to brown. Remove to wire rack and sift castor sugar over the top while still warm.
Makes 22-24

Ginger-glazed Shortbread; Shortbread Pennies; Melt-away Shortbread.

SPICY SHORTBREAD

This shortbread is made with oil.

400 ml cake flour
100 ml cornflour
1 ml salt
5 ml grated nutmeg (scant)
125 ml castor sugar
150 ml oil

TOPPING
5 ml castor sugar mixed with
a pinch ground cinnamon

Sift dry ingredients together. Add oil and knead until smooth. Press the dough evenly onto the ungreased base of a 22 cm-diameter, loose-bottomed cake tin. Use a rolling pin to flatten evenly. Mark into 12 wedges, prick well, crimp edges, and sprinkle with topping. Leave to stand about 30 minutes. Bake at 150 °C for 45 minutes. Cut right through wedges, but leave to stand on base until cold and crisp.
Makes 12 wedges

MOCHA PECAN SHORTBREAD

Deliciously different.

125 g soft butter
60 ml castor sugar
10 ml instant coffee granules
10 ml water
300 ml cake flour
50 ml cornflour
50-75 ml finely chopped pecan nuts

Using an electric beater, cream butter. Slowly add sugar, beating until light and fluffy. Beat in coffee dissolved in water. Sift flour with cornflour and add slowly, beating all the time. When mixture becomes moist and starts to form a ball, add nuts and knead well. Press into ungreased 18 x 18 cm baking tin, prick well and mark into 18 fingers. Bake on middle shelf of oven at 150 °C for 45 minutes. Cut through fingers and leave in tin until cold.
Makes 18

MELT-AWAY SHORTBREAD

A basic flop-proof recipe.

250 g soft butter
125 ml castor sugar
600 ml cake flour
150 ml cornflour
extra castor sugar

Cream the butter, then slowly add the sugar, beating well until pale and fluffy. Sift together the flour and cornflour and slowly beat into the butter mixture to make a soft and creamy dough. Press evenly into an ungreased, 33 x 20 cm Swiss roll tin. Prick well, mark lightly into fingers, and then bake at 150 °C for 45 minutes until it becomes a pale biscuit colour. Remove from oven and cut the shortbread into fingers along markings. Sprinkle lightly with castor sugar and leave in tin until cold. Remove and store in airtight container.
Makes 30

YEAST BREADS

WHITE FARMHOUSE BREAD

Instant yeast reduces the rising time of bread, and I have used it here to make a high, attractive flour-topped loaf. The 'farmhouse' effect comes from slashing the unbaked loaf lengthwise – as it rises in the oven the slashes open out. Baked in a smaller tin than usual, the result is a loaf with a high, humped fan-like top. However, the dough may be used in more conventional ways if preferred.

10 ml instant dry yeast
4 x 250 ml white bread flour
7 ml salt
7 ml sugar
25 ml butter
325 ml warm water

In a large bowl mix yeast, flour sifted with salt, and sugar. Rub in butter. Add water. Mix, first with a wooden spoon and then with the hands to make a kneadable dough, adding about 20 ml extra warm water if necessary. Knead in the bowl for about 5 minutes, until soft and pliable, then cover bowl with a damp cloth and leave to rest for 30 minutes in a warm place. Oil a 20 x 9 x 7 cm loaf tin.

Punch dough down and form into a loaf by pressing dough out to the length of the tin, and three times the width. Fold over, sides to middle, and drop into tin, seam side down. Press dough out evenly into the corners. Cover loosely with oiled plastic wrap and leave to rise for 30 minutes until dough reaches just over the top of the tin. Using a sharp knife, make several deep slits lengthwise along the top of the loaf and sift over a little flour. Bake on middle shelf of oven at 200 °C for 30 minutes until well-risen, and the slashes have burst open. Turn out onto wire rack to cool completely.

Makes 1 loaf

Italian Herbed Bread (page 39); Cheese-topped Onion Crown Loaf (page 40); White Farmhouse Bread; Baker's Pride Bread (page 39).

BASIC WHITE BREAD

Baking one's own bread is one of the ultimate culinary pleasures. From the fermenting of the yeast and the magical rising of the dough, to the final, aromatic waft of a billowing, crusty loaf, it is a matchless feeling of achievement and a wonderful eating experience. However, yeast breads cannot be hurried. A good rising, especially the second one, is vital.

7 x 250 ml white bread flour
10 ml salt
30 ml butter
10 ml sugar
625 ml warm water
15 ml dried yeast

GLAZE
1 egg white lightly mixed with
5 ml water

Sift flour and salt into a large bowl. Rub in butter. Dissolve sugar in 250 ml of the water. Sprinkle in the yeast, cover and leave about 10 minutes until frothy. Pour yeast mixture in a well in centre of flour, mix, and add remaining water. Mix to a dough – you may need just a little extra water. Turn onto a lightly floured board. Knead very well, about 10 minutes, until smooth and elastic. Brush a large bowl with oil, turn the dough in it to coat, cover and leave to rise in a warm place for about 1½ hours until doubled. (To test, press the risen dough deeply with one finger – the dent should remain.)

Punch down and knead briefly, then break off two-thirds of the dough. Knead into a loaf and place in oiled 23 x 8 x 7 cm loaf tin. Brush top with glaze, cover lightly and leave about 1½ hours or until dough reaches to 2 cm above top of tin. Brush again with glaze and bake at 220 °C for 15 minutes. Reduce heat to 200 °C and bake another 35 minutes. Turn out onto wire rack – if you rap the bottom of the loaf, it should sound hollow. Leave to cool.

To make a Vienna Double Plait, roll remaining dough into six long sausages of equal length. Make two plaits, place one on top of the other, dampen ends and pinch to seal. Cover lightly and leave to rise for about 1½ hours until doubled. Place on oiled baking tray, brush with milk, sprinkle with poppy seeds and bake at 220 °C for 10 minutes, then at 180 °C for 20 minutes. Break into chunks to serve.

Makes 2 loaves

HERBED WHITE BREAD BRAID

For extra lightness use half white bread flour and half cake flour.

7 x 250 ml sifted white bread flour
10 ml salt
25 ml melted butter
100 ml chopped parsley
1 small onion, finely chopped
5 ml dried thyme
2 cloves garlic, crushed
10 ml sugar
about 600 ml warm water
15 ml dried yeast
grated Parmesan cheese and poppy seeds

Sift flour with salt. Add butter, parsley, onion, thyme and garlic. Stir sugar into 250 ml of the water, sprinkle in the yeast, cover and leave until frothy. Pour yeast mixture into a well in the flour, mix and add remaining water or enough to make a workable dough. Knead until smooth and elastic. Shape into a ball and place in bowl. Brush top with oil, cover and leave to rise in a warm place until doubled, about 45 minutes.

Punch down, knead well (the dough should feel springy and alive) and then divide into two. Divide each half into three, roll into long sausages and then plait, pinching to close at both ends. Place loaves on oiled baking trays, cover lightly with damp cloth and leave to rise until doubled – 30-60 minutes. Brush with milk and sprinkle with Parmesan and poppy seeds. Bake at 220 °C for 10 minutes, then reduce heat to 180 °C and bake 20 minutes longer. Break into chunks to serve.

Makes 2 large braids

KITKE

This recipe makes a beautifully big, rich white braid, but it requires three risings, so allow plenty of time.

250 ml warm water
30 ml sugar
10 ml dried yeast
4 x 250 ml white bread flour
5 ml salt
25 ml oil
2 eggs, beaten
poppy seeds

Pour 60 ml of the water into a mug. Stir in 5 ml of the sugar and then sprinkle in the yeast. Cover and leave to froth. Sift flour and salt. Add remaining 25 ml sugar. Quickly stir yeast mixture and pour into a well in the centre of the flour mixture. Stir to mix, then add oil, eggs and remaining 190 ml warm water. Mix to a workable dough – you may need a dash more water. Turn onto floured board and knead for 10 minutes until very smooth and pale khaki in colour. Shape into a ball, brush a bowl with oil and turn dough in it until coated. Cover and leave to rise until doubled, about 1¼ hours.

Punch down, cover and leave to rise again until doubled. Divide dough into three, roll into 40 cm-long sausages, and plait. Pinch ends firmly together and place on oiled baking tray. Cover loosely with oiled plastic wrap and leave to rise until doubled, about 45 minutes. Brush with milk and sprinkle with poppy seeds. Bake just above centre of oven at 200 °C for 10 minutes, then at 180 °C for 20 minutes. Carefully transfer to wire rack to cool.

Makes 1 loaf

FRENCH BREAD

Most home-bakers cannot produce those typical French baguettes. The technique differs from that of ordinary bread, and the equipment can be quite daunting. This fairly quick and easy recipe will produce two fine loaves or bâtards. French bread contains no sugar, butter or oil, so eat it on the day of baking.

15 ml dried yeast
400 ml warm water
625 ml cake flour
625 ml white bread flour
5 ml salt
sesame seeds

Sprinkle yeast into 125 ml of the water, cover and leave 15 minutes until frothy. Sift flours and salt into a large bowl. Stir yeast and pour into well in centre of sifted mixture. Mix, then slowly add rest of water to make a fairly soft dough. Another 5-10 ml water may be necessary. Knead vigorously for 10 minutes on lightly floured board. Return to bowl, cover loosely with a damp cloth and leave to rise in a warm place for about 2 hours or until just more than doubled. Prod with two fingers – the indentations should remain. Knock down and knead hard for a few minutes – the dough should be springy and alive.

Divide into two balls, cover and stand 10 minutes. Roll balls into two 37 cm-long sausages and place on floured cloth. Tuck cloth up tightly against sides to prevent loaves from spreading sideways. Cover loosely with another cloth and leave to rise for 1-1½ hours until nearly doubled in height.

Without touching the loaves, roll them over very gently onto a non-stick baking tray so that they lie upside down. Remove any traces of flour with pastry brush. Slash tops three times diagonally, brush with water and sprinkle with sesame seeds. For a shiny, crisp crust, place pan of boiling water at bottom of a 220 °C pre-heated oven. Bake loaves just above centre of oven for 15 minutes. Reduce heat to 180 °C and bake for 20 minutes. Cool on a wire rack.

Makes 2 loaves

WHITE RING BREAD

Similar to the Greek Kouloura *Ring, this is a plain but attractive loaf, baked in a tube tin and rising into a high ring, strewn with poppy seeds and with a nice brown crust.*

20 ml sugar
60 ml warm water
10 ml dried yeast
250 ml milk
20 ml butter
1 egg, beaten
750 ml white bread flour
5 ml salt
poppy seeds

Dissolve 5 ml of the sugar in the water, sprinkle in the yeast, cover and leave to froth. Meanwhile scald the milk, add butter and remaining 15 ml sugar and cool to lukewarm. Stir in egg, reserving 5 ml. Sift flour with salt into mixing bowl. Stir frothy yeast and pour into a well in the centre of the flour. Mix, then add milk mixture and combine well to a very soft dough. Turn onto well-floured board and knead for 10 minutes, adding about 60 ml extra flour in stages, as it becomes necessary. When dough is smooth and pliable and no longer sticky, shape into a ball and place in oiled bowl, turning to coat. Cover and leave to rise until doubled, about 1¼ hours.

Punch down and knead for about 1 minute, then roll into a long, smooth sausage. Coil the sausage in oiled, 20 cm-diameter x 7 cm-deep spring tube tin, joining ends firmly by first brushing with a little of the reserved beaten egg. Press dough down evenly – the tin should be half full. Cover and leave until dough has risen to just over the top – about 1¼ hours. Brush top with remaining egg and sprinkle liberally with poppy seeds. Place a pan of hot water on bottom shelf of oven, and bake bread at 200 °C for 10 minutes. Cover the top loosely with a sheet of greaseproof paper and bake for a further 30 minutes at 180 °C. Release the spring of the tin and turn out to cool on wire rack.

Makes 1 loaf

Italian Herbed Bread

A fragrant round loaf, baked in a cake tin. This is not a standard bread dough, and it takes longer to rise than usual, but the reward is in the eating. Break into crusty chunks, and serve warm with butter and a bowl of hot soup.

5 ml sugar
60 ml warm water
10 ml dried yeast
125 ml milk
25 ml butter
1 egg, beaten
750 ml white bread flour
5 ml salt
75 ml finely chopped parsley
2-3 large cloves garlic, crushed
4 spring onions, plus some of the tops, chopped
5 ml dried origanum
25 ml grated Parmesan cheese

Stir sugar into water, sprinkle in yeast, cover and leave to froth. Scald milk, remove from stove, add butter and when melted stir in egg. Cool to lukewarm. Sift 500 ml of the flour together with the salt into a bowl. Stir the bubbly yeast and pour into a well in the centre of the flour mixture. Mix and add milk mixture. Stir in parsley, garlic, spring onions and origanum. When well combined, sift in remaining 250 ml flour. Mix with hands until dough holds together and then turn out onto a floured board and knead 5-10 minutes until the dough becomes a pliable ball. Brush bowl with oil and turn dough in it to coat, then cover and leave until well risen, about 2 hours.

Punch down and knead lightly. Place in a 20 cm-diameter, 6 cm-deep oiled cake tin, pressing the dough vigorously with your fingers to spread it out to the sides in a flat, level cake. The tin should be a third full. Cover with a cloth and leave to rise for 1½ hours or until dough fills two thirds of tin. Brush with milk and sprinkle with Parmesan, then bake on middle shelf at 200 °C for 10 minutes, then at 180 °C for 25 minutes. Turn out onto wire rack.

Makes 1 loaf

Italian Herbed Bread and Baker's Pride Bread are both delicious with soup.

Baker's Pride Bread

A big, savoury loaf, so easy to make, but really impressive.

4 x 250 ml white bread flour
10 ml instant dry yeast
5 ml salt
7 ml mixed dried herbs
1 small onion, finely chopped
100 ml chopped parsley
10 ml sugar
15 ml oil
450 ml warm water
caraway seeds

Mix flour, yeast, salt, herbs, onion, parsley and sugar in large mixing bowl. Stir oil into water and add to flour mixture. Mix well to a tacky batter, then turn into an oiled 23 x 8 x 7 cm loaf tin. The batter will be quite headstrong and elastic – use a dampened rubber spatula to press it in evenly. Sprinkle top with caraway seeds and leave to rise in a warm place, uncovered, until dough rises to just above the top of the tin – 35-45 minutes. Bake at 200 °C for 30 minutes, then at 180 °C for another 30 minutes. Turn out and cool on wire rack.

Makes 1 large loaf

Cheese-topped Onion Crown Loaf

A novelty savoury bread, light in texture and beautiful in appearance. Balls of dough are arranged in a cake tin for proving, where they join into a circle of buns with humped tops – hence the name 'crown'.

5 ml sugar
200 ml warm water
7 ml dried yeast
500 ml white bread flour
5 ml salt
250 ml wholewheat flour
1 large onion, finely chopped and sautéed in a little oil
100 ml finely chopped parsley
15 ml butter

TOPPING
75 ml finely grated Cheddar cheese
plenty of milled black pepper

Stir sugar into water, sprinkle in yeast, cover and leave to froth. Sift white flour with salt. Add wholewheat flour, onion and parsley. Rub in butter. Stir frothy yeast and pour into well in centre of dry ingredients. Mix to a dough, first with a wooden spoon and then with the hands. Turn onto floured board and knead for 5 minutes to a soft and elastic ball. Place in oiled bowl, turn to coat, then cover and leave to rise until doubled, about 1 hour.

Punch down, cover and rest 10 minutes. Divide into 6 pieces and roll each into a smooth ball. Place 5 of the balls in a ring around the sides of an oiled 20 cm-diameter x 6 cm-deep cake tin, spacing them equally. Place the sixth ball in the centre. Cover loosely with oiled plastic wrap and leave to prove for about 45 minutes, until rolls reach top of tin and are all joined together. Brush with milk, sprinkle with cheese and grind the pepper over. Bake just above centre of oven at 200 °C for 10 minutes, then at 180 °C for 35 minutes. Run a knife round the circumference and turn onto wire rack to cool. Serve by breaking buns apart.
Makes 1 loaf

Cheese and Caraway Cottage Loaf

Making this quaintly-shaped loaf is pure pleasure. It is lightly flavoured with caraway and enriched with cheese and skimmed milk powder which may be omitted if a lighter-textured loaf is required.

10 ml sugar
350 ml warm water
10 ml dried yeast
4 x 250 ml white bread flour
10 ml salt
10 ml dry mustard
100 ml skimmed milk powder
5 ml caraway seeds
300 ml finely grated Cheddar cheese

Mix sugar into water, sprinkle in yeast, cover and leave to froth. Sift flour, salt, mustard and milk powder. Add caraway seeds and 250 ml of the cheese. Stir risen yeast and pour into well in centre of dry ingredients. Mix well, adding about 10 ml warm water to make a kneadable dough. Turn onto lightly floured board and knead for 5-8 minutes until smooth and elastic. Place in bowl brushed with oil, turn to coat, cover and leave to rise for 1¼ - 1½ hours until doubled. (Due to the extra ingredients this dough has a slow rising period.)

Punch down, cover and rest 10 minutes. Pinch off three-quarters of the dough and shape it into a flat 18 cm-diameter circle, using a rolling pin to get it really smooth. Brush with milk. Form the remaining piece of dough into a ball and place on top of the base. Push the handle of a wooden spoon right through the centre, from the top to the bottom, to keep the ball in place. Remove spoon and place loaf in an oiled 21 x 21 cm square tin to prevent base from spreading too much, cover loosely with oiled plastic wrap and leave to prove about 45 minutes until doubled. Brush with milk, sprinkle with remaining cheese, and bake on middle shelf of oven at 200 °C for 30 minutes. Cover it loosely with greaseproof paper if over-browning. Cool on wire rack.
Makes 1 loaf

Spiced Fruit Braid

125 ml seedless raisins
100 ml currants
50 ml mixed peel
25 ml dark rum
25 ml sugar
125 ml warm water
10 ml dried yeast
625 ml white bread flour
2 ml salt
2 ml ground mixed spice
5 ml ground cinnamon
25 ml butter
1 egg, beaten

GLAZE
5 ml sugar
10 ml boiling water

Place fruit in small bowl, add rum, stir to mix, then cover and stand for 1 hour. In another small bowl mix sugar into water, sprinkle in the yeast, cover and leave to froth.

In a large bowl sift flour, salt and spices. Rub in butter. Add egg to frothy yeast, mix well, then pour into well in centre of dry ingredients. Stir until flour is thoroughly moistened, then knead hard for 5-10 minutes. Cover and rest dough for 10 minutes, then add soaked fruit. At first this seems like too much fruit, but keep kneading and eventually it will all be taken up by the dough, leaving the sides of the bowl quite clean. Cover and leave to rise in a warm place until doubled, about 1½ hours.

Punch down and divide into three. Roll each portion out into a 40 cm-long sausage. Make a plait, tucking the ends under, and place on oiled baking tray. Cover lightly and leave to rise in a warm place for about 1 hour or until doubled in volume.

Bake at 220 °C for 10 minutes, then reduce heat to 180 °C and bake for another 20 minutes, covering the top loosely with a sheet of foil, shiny side out, when sufficiently browned. Remove to wire rack to cool, and glaze while warm, not hot. To make the glaze, dissolve sugar in the water and brush over the top of the loaf.
Makes 1 loaf

Swedish Tea Ring

125 ml milk
50 ml butter
7 ml dried yeast
50 ml warm water
50 ml castor sugar
1 egg, beaten
600 ml cake flour
2 ml salt

FILLING
20 ml melted butter
30 ml castor sugar
125 ml fruit cake mix
6 glacé cherries, chopped
2 ml ground cinnamon
2 ml ground mixed spice

Scald milk, add butter and cool to lukewarm. Sprinkle yeast into water, cover and leave to froth. Stir sugar and egg into milk mixture. Sift flour and salt, stir yeast and pour into well in centre of flour. Add liquid and mix to a soft dough. Knead on a floured board for 5-8 minutes, slowly adding extra flour as necessary until dough becomes smooth and pliable. Return to bowl, brush top with oil, cover with a damp cloth and leave to rise in a warm place for about 1 hour 20 minutes or until doubled.

Punch down, knead 1 minute, cover and leave to rise again for 30 minutes. Roll out on floured board to a large rectangle, about 4 mm thick. Brush entire surface with melted butter. Sprinkle with sugar, fruit and spices, then roll up tightly, like a Swiss roll. Curve into a ring, about 21 cm in diameter, joining ends firmly together with dampened fingers. Lift carefully with a spatula onto an oiled baking tray. Using kitchen scissors, snip top at 3 cm intervals, cutting half way through dough. Cover loosely with oiled plastic wrap and leave until well risen, about 45 minutes.

Bake on middle shelf of oven at 200 °C for 10 minutes, then at 180 °C for 15 minutes. Place greaseproof paper over the top when lightly browned. Cool for a few minutes on the tray so as not to break ring when transferring to wire rack. Ice and decorate when cold.

Makes 1 ring loaf

A colourful Swedish Tea Ring and Spiced Fruit Braid to grace the tea table.

HEALTH
BREADS

Nutty Brown Bloomer Loaf

A beautiful bread, as professional-looking as anything you can buy. It requires only one rising, which is quite lengthy due to the unrefined ingredients, but is still easy to make and is tops on the taste test.

750 ml wholewheat flour
10 ml salt
15 ml instant dry yeast
350 ml warm water
25 ml honey
25 ml oil
500 ml white bread flour
125 ml wheat germ
125 ml sunflower seeds

In a large mixing bowl combine 375 ml of the wholewheat flour, salt and instant yeast. Mix together water, honey and oil. Stir into flour mixture and mix to a sloppy dough. Cover and rest 10 minutes. Add remaining 375 ml wholewheat flour, white flour, wheat germ and sunflower seeds. Mix with a wooden spoon and then with the hands to form a dough, adding up to 75 ml extra warm water as necessary. Knead in the bowl for 8-10 minutes – this is a firm dough which requires some hard kneading. When mixture forms a smooth ball and leaves the sides of the bowl clean, shape into a 25 x 12 cm bloomer (or slab) with blunt ends.

Place on oiled baking tray, and tuck two cloths tightly on either side so that the dough rises upwards rather than sideways. Make six deep diagonal slashes across the top, then cover loosely with oiled plastic wrap and leave to rise for about 1 hour or until doubled. Brush with milk and bake on middle shelf of oven at 200 °C for 30 minutes. Cool on wire rack, and brush top with melted butter for a shiny finish.

Makes 1 loaf

FROM THE BACK: *Nutty Brown Bloomer Loaf; Caraway Rye Loaf (page 46); Herbed Brown Bread Plait; Buttermilk Wholewheat Soda Bread with Rosemary (page 44).*

Herbed Brown Bread Plait

This is a rewarding bread to bake, rising beautifully to a fat and chunky plait, topped with crushed wheat and lightly flavoured with herbs. The addition of a little soya flour is optional, but it adds nutrition and helps to keep the loaf fresh. Break into chunks to serve.

300 ml warm water
10 ml dried yeast
500 ml white bread flour
500 ml wholewheat flour
50 ml soya flour (optional)
10 ml dried mixed herbs
5 ml salt
25 ml oil
25 ml honey

TOPPING
30 ml crushed wheat
1 ml mixed dried herbs

Pour 125 ml of the water into a mug. Sprinkle in yeast, cover and leave to froth. Mix white bread, wholewheat and soya flours in large bowl. Add herbs, salt, oil and honey. Stir the risen yeast and pour into a well in centre of dry ingredients. Add remaining 175 ml water, or just enough to make a workable dough. Turn onto floured board and knead well for 10 minutes, re-flouring the board when necessary – the dough is inclined to be sticky. When it forms a smooth ball, place in bowl brushed with oil, turn to coat, cover and leave to rise until doubled, about 1-1½ hours.

Punch down, cover and leave to rest for 10 minutes. Divide dough into three and roll into 36 cm-long sausages. Make a plait, pinching ends to join firmly. Cover the plait loosely with a piece of oiled plastic wrap and leave to prove until it has doubled in volume, about 45 minutes. Brush top with milk and sprinkle with crushed wheat and herbs. Bake just above centre of oven at 200 °C for 10 minutes, then at 180 °C for 20 minutes. Cool on wire rack.

Makes 1 loaf

Wholewheat Batons with Garlic and Fresh Herbs

These French-style batons have a marvellous flavour, and are excellent with soups, cheese or pâté. It should not be sliced, but broken into chunks.

10 ml honey
300 ml warm water
10 ml dried yeast
500 ml white bread flour
5 ml salt
500 ml wholewheat flour
4 cloves garlic, crushed
50 ml finely chopped parsley
5 ml chopped fresh rosemary needles
10 fresh sage leaves, chopped
5 ml finely chopped fresh origanum leaves
beaten egg, sesame and poppy seeds

Dissolve honey in water. Sprinkle in the yeast, cover and leave to froth. Sift white flour with salt into a large bowl. Add wholewheat flour, garlic, and all the herbs and mix well. Pour frothy yeast into a well in the centre and work in the flour until incorporated. Turn onto lightly floured board and knead hard for 10 minutes. Shape into a ball, return to bowl, brush top with oil, cover and leave to rise in a warm place for about 1½ hours or until doubled.

Punch down and divide into two. Shape each piece into a 28 cm-long baton and place on an oiled baking tray. With a sharp knife slash tops three times, diagonally, and leave to rise until nearly doubled, about 1¼ hours. Brush with beaten egg and sprinkle with sesame and poppy seeds in alternate, diagonal stripes. Bake just above centre of oven at 220 °C for 10 minutes, then at 180 °C for 15 minutes. Cool on wire rack.

Makes 2 loaves

HINT
- *Remember to remove the oiled plastic wrap on top of a risen loaf before baking.*

Wholewheat Nut, Raisin and Yoghurt Bread

Too dense for a tea loaf, too spicy for a bread, but a superb, nutritious snack-time loaf.

250 ml white bread flour
5 ml salt
7 ml bicarbonate of soda
5 ml ground cinnamon
2 ml grated nutmeg
1 ml ground cloves
750 ml wholewheat flour
25 ml oil
25 ml honey
50 ml light brown sugar
125 ml seedless raisins
100-125 ml finely chopped walnuts, pecan or Brazil nuts
500 ml natural drinking yoghurt

TOPPING
2 ml ground cinnamon
25 ml light brown sugar

Sift white flour with salt, bicarbonate of soda and spices. Mix in wholewheat flour, oil, honey, sugar, raisins and nuts. Stir in yoghurt, using a wooden spoon. Rinse the carton with 25 ml water and add. Mix ingredients thoroughly, then turn batter into an oiled 26 x 9 x 7 cm loaf tin, spreading evenly. Sprinkle cinnamon and sugar over the top, and bake on middle shelf of oven at 180 °C for 1 hour. Stand 5 minutes before turning out onto wire rack to cool.
Makes 1 loaf

HINT
- *Be wary of adding too much water to a batter bread. If you make it too wet, the loaf will deflate in the oven. The consistency should be fairly thick and moist, like a fruit cake mixture.*
- *Baking bread with a pan of water placed low down in the oven will produce a crisp crust.*

Wholewheat Honey Bread

1 x 10 g packet instant dry yeast
100 ml wheat germ
4 x 250 ml wholewheat flour
125 ml seedless raisins
5 ml salt
100 ml sunflower seeds
approximately 500 ml warm water
50 ml honey
15 ml oil

Mix yeast, wheat germ, flour, raisins, salt and sunflower seeds in a large bowl. Whisk 250 ml of the water with honey and oil. Add to dry ingredients, mix, then add remaining 250 ml water, or enough to make a batter with the consistency of a fruit cake. Turn into an oiled 23 x 8 x 7 cm loaf tin, and cover loosely with oiled plastic wrap. Leave in a warm place until batter rises to just over the top of the tin – about 30 minutes. Bake at 200 °C for 30 minutes, then reduce heat to 180 °C and bake for 20 minutes. Turn out onto wire rack to cool.
Makes 1 large loaf

Buttermilk Wholewheat Soda Bread with Rosemary

Soda bread is a traditional Scottish bread, served on Burns Night, with Finnan Haddie Soup and Haggis. I have added fresh rosemary, which makes a lovely, perfumed bread. Serve freshly baked, broken into quarters, with butter.

500 ml cake flour
5 ml salt
5 ml bicarbonate of soda
5 ml sugar
500 ml wholewheat flour
15 ml finely chopped fresh rosemary needles
25 ml butter
about 400 ml buttermilk

Sift cake flour with salt and bicarbonate of soda. Add sugar, wholewheat flour and rosemary. Rub in butter. Add buttermilk and mix to a soft dough. Shape into two 15 cm-diameter rounds, and place on a floured baking tray. Using the back of a knife, score deeply into quarters. Brush tops with beaten egg (milk may be used, but egg gives a better colour) and bake at 200 °C for 30 minutes.
Makes 2 loaves

Enriched Batter Bread

A delicious loaf, packed with healthy ingredients. It rises well, has an even, flat top, and slices neatly.

25 ml honey
475 ml warm water
10 ml dried yeast
750 ml wholewheat flour
125 ml crushed wheat
75 ml soya flour
75 ml fat-free milk powder
100 ml wheat germ
250 ml brown bread flour
7 ml salt
25 ml oil
sunflower seeds

Dissolve honey in 125 ml of the water. Sprinkle in the yeast, cover and leave to froth. Mix remaining ingredients (except sunflower seeds). Give the frothy yeast a quick stir and pour into a well in centre of dry ingredients. Mix, using a wooden spoon, and gradually add the remaining 350 ml water, or just enough to give you a thick, sticky batter. Turn into an oiled 26 x 9 x 7 cm loaf tin, which should be nearly two-thirds full. Sprinkle the top thickly with sunflower seeds, pressing them in lightly. Cover loosely with oiled plastic wrap and leave to rise in a warm place for 45-60 minutes. Bake on middle shelf of oven at 200 °C for 15 minutes, then at 180 °C for 45-60 minutes. Stand a few minutes, run a knife round edges and turn out onto wire rack to cool.
Makes 1 loaf

Pumpernickel Bread

This is an unusual dark bread made with a variety of flours and interesting ingredients which could include mashed potato, caraway seeds, chocolate and coffee powder. The following is a delectable, fairly sweet version, containing a sprinkling of fruit, honey and molasses, with the cocoa and coffee providing colour rather than flavour.

300 ml warm water
25 ml molasses
50 ml thin honey
10 ml dried yeast
10 ml instant coffee granules
10 ml salt
15 ml cocoa powder
25 ml melted butter
375 ml rye flour
375 ml white bread flour
250 ml wholewheat flour
50 ml seedless raisins
50 ml currants

GLAZE
1 egg white mixed with 10 ml water

In a large bowl mix water, molasses and honey. When dissolved, sprinkle in the yeast, cover and stand in a warm place until mixture begins to bubble, about 15 minutes. Stir in coffee, salt, cocoa and butter and when smoothly mixed add the flours, one by one. Mix to a dough, turn onto a lightly floured board and knead vigorously for 10 minutes until smooth and pliable. Place in a bowl brushed with oil, turn to coat dough on all sides, then cover bowl with plastic wrap, leaving plenty of room for air and rising. Leave in a warm place until nearly trebled in bulk, 2-2½ hours. To test, prod the dough with one finger and if the indentation remains, it is ready.

Punch down, add raisins and currants and knead hard for 5 minutes. Shape into a large round, place on oiled baking tray which has been dusted with cornflour, cover lightly and leave to rise for 1½-2 hours, or until doubled in bulk. Brush with glaze and bake at 200 °C for 50-60 minutes. The bread will be very dark and shiny, and should sound hollow when rapped on the bottom. Cool on wire rack and cut into thin slices.

Makes 1 large loaf

Wholewheat Nut, Raisin and Yoghurt Bread, a superb, nutritious snack-time loaf to serve with cheese, cold meats or pâté.

CARAWAY RYE LOAF

A soft, malt-coloured loaf, subtly flavoured with caraway, made in a baton shape. Good with cheese, cold meats, mustard and pickles.

25 ml molasses
200 ml warm water
10 ml dried yeast
250 ml white bread flour
250 ml wholewheat flour
250 ml rye flour
5 ml salt
25 ml oil
5 ml caraway seeds

Dissolve molasses in water. Sprinkle in yeast, cover and leave to froth. Meanwhile mix remaining ingredients except caraway seeds. Stir yeast, and pour into well in centre of dry ingredients. Mix to a dough. You might have to add about 10 ml extra warm water. Turn onto a lightly floured board and knead for 10 minutes until smooth. The dough will be firm, rather than spongy. Brush a bowl with oil, turn the dough round in bowl to coat, then cover and leave to rise for about 1½ hours until doubled.

Punch down and knead in caraway seeds until well distributed. Shape into a 22 cm-long baton, and place on an oiled baking tray. Make three deep diagonal slashes on the top, cover loosely with oiled plastic wrap and leave to rise for about 45 minutes or until doubled – the dough will rise both upwards and sideways. Brush top with milk and sprinkle with extra caraway seeds, or sift over a little rye flour. Bake on middle shelf of oven at 200 °C for 10 minutes, then at 180 °C for 25-30 minutes. Cool on a wire rack.

Makes 1 loaf

> NOTE
> - *Doughs containing rye flour are always a little sticky.*
> - *If bread dough has risen before the oven is ready, immediately remove to a cool place and uncover.*

CHEESE, ONION AND GARLIC BATTER BREAD

Delicious with pâté or cheese, or simply buttered.

10 ml instant dry yeast
375 ml white bread flour
375 ml wholewheat flour
5 ml salt
10 ml sugar
2 cloves garlic, crushed
125 ml finely grated Cheddar cheese
1 small onion, finely chopped
50 ml chopped parsley
25 ml butter
approximately 350 ml warm water
sesame seeds

Mix yeast, both flours, salt, sugar, garlic, cheese, onion and parsley. Rub in butter. Stir in just enough water to make a thick, porridge-like batter. Turn into an oiled 20 x 9 x 7 cm loaf tin, sprinkle with sesame seeds, and cover very lightly with oiled plastic wrap. Leave to rise in a warm place for about 30 minutes or until doubled. Bake at 200 °C for 30 minutes and then at 180 °C for 30 minutes. When sufficiently browned, cover top lightly with a sheet of greaseproof paper. Stand a few minutes before turning out, and then return to oven, upside down, for 5 minutes to crisp the sides. Cool on wire rack.

Makes 1 loaf

INSTANT WHOLEWHEAT BATTER BREAD

The perfect bread for reluctant bakers.

750 ml wholewheat flour
250 ml white bread flour
100 ml crushed wheat
10 ml instant yeast
5 ml salt
100 ml sunflower seeds
25 ml oil
25 ml honey
approximately 450 ml warm water
extra sunflower seeds

Mix flours, crushed wheat, yeast, salt and sunflower seeds. Mix in oil and honey. Add 300 ml of the water, then stir in just enough of the remaining water to make a soft, sticky dough. Mix well, then turn into an oiled 23 x 9 x 8 cm loaf tin, sprinkle with sunflower seeds, pressing in lightly, and leave to rise in a warm place until 1-2 cm over top of tin. Cover, if liked, with a large plastic bag, allowing it to balloon over the top so that it does not stick to the rising dough. Bake on middle shelf of oven at 200 °C for 30 minutes and then at 180 °C for 30 minutes. Cool on wire rack.

Makes 1 medium loaf

FOUR-SEED BATTER BREAD

A nutritious, crunchy, flat-topped loaf, excellent for sandwiches as it slices so well.

25 ml honey
550 ml warm water
15 ml dried yeast
4 x 250 ml wholewheat flour
250 ml white bread flour
50 ml sesame seeds
100 ml sunflower seeds
50 ml linseeds
5 ml salt
poppy seeds

Mix honey into 250 ml of the warm water and stir to dissolve. Sprinkle in the yeast, cover and leave to froth. Mix flours, sesame seeds, sunflower seeds, linseeds and salt. Stir risen yeast, pour into a well in centre of flour mixture, stir, then slowly add the remaining 300 ml water, or just enough to make a sticky but quite stiff dough. Pat firmly into an oiled 26 x 9 x 7 cm loaf tin, sprinkle with poppy seeds and leave to rise in a warm place for 1 hour, or until just over the top of the tin. Bake at 200 °C for 30 minutes, and then at 180 °C for 30 minutes. Run a knife round the sides and leave in tin for 1 minute before turning out onto a wire rack to cool.

Makes 1 loaf

Herbed Oat Batter Bread

about 375 ml warm water
5 ml sugar
10 ml dried yeast
400 ml wholewheat flour
200 ml white bread flour
200 ml crushed wheat
250 ml rolled oats
5 ml salt
3-4 cloves garlic, crushed
25 ml finely chopped fresh rosemary needles
25 ml oil
25 ml honey

Pour 250 ml of the water into a jug. Stir in sugar, sprinkle in the yeast, then cover and stand until frothy, about 15 minutes. Mix flours, crushed wheat, oats, salt, garlic and rosemary. Stir oil and honey into yeast mixture, then add to flour mixture. Mix, and then slowly stir in remaining 125 ml water or enough to make a sloppy dough. When well combined, turn into oiled 20 x 9 x 7 cm loaf tin. Smooth the top, then leave to rise in a warm place until 1 cm over the top of the tin – about 45 minutes. Bake at 200 °C for 30 minutes, then at 180 °C for 20-25 minutes. Stand for 1 minute, run a knife round the edges and turn out onto a wire rack to cool. Brush top with melted butter.
Makes 1 loaf

A crunchy slice of Instant Wholewheat Batter Bread or Nutty Wholewheat Batter Bread goes well with a crisp salad.

Nutty Wholewheat Batter Bread

Excellent with pâtés or cheese.

500-600 ml warm water
15 ml honey
10 ml dried yeast
4 x 250 ml wholewheat flour
250 ml white bread flour
7 ml salt
15 ml oil
100 ml sunflower seeds
100 ml linseeds
extra sunflower seeds

Mix 250 ml of the water with the honey and stir until dissolved. Sprinkle yeast on top, cover and leave until frothy, about 10 minutes. Mix wholewheat and white flours, salt and oil. Stir in yeast mixture, sunflower seeds and linseeds. Add rest of water, or as much as is necessary to make a soft dough. Spoon into an oiled and floured 23 x 8 x 7 cm loaf tin, patting in firmly. Sprinkle the top with extra sunflower seeds and leave to rise in a warm place for about 1 hour, or until dough rises to 2 cm above the top of the tin. Bake at 200 °C for 45 minutes. Run a knife round the edges, turn out and cool on wire rack before slicing.
Makes 1 fairly large loaf

ROLLS & RUSKS

WHITE ROLLS

10 ml sugar
125 ml warm water
10 ml dried yeast
125 ml milk
15 ml butter
4 x 250 ml cake flour
7 ml salt
1 egg, beaten

Stir sugar into water, sprinkle in yeast, cover and leave to froth. Scald milk, add butter and leave until lukewarm. Sift flour and salt into a large bowl. Stir yeast, pour into well in centre of flour, and mix. Beat egg with cooled milk mixture and add all at once to flour mixture. Mix to a kneadable dough, adding about 25 ml extra warm water if necessary. Turn onto lightly floured board and knead for 10 minutes until pliable and smooth. Shape into a ball, put back in oiled bowl, turn to coat, cover and rise for 1-1½ hours until doubled.

Punch down, cover and rest for 5-10 minutes. Shape and place on oiled baking trays. Prove for 30-40 minutes until virtually doubled. Brush with milk, sprinkle with suggested toppings, and bake just above centre of oven at 220 °C for 10 minutes, then at 180 °C for 5 minutes. (Brushing with milk provides a light golden colour; egg-wash may be used but be careful of over-browning.)
Makes 12 large rolls

Rolls
Roll into balls. Brush with milk and sprinkle with sesame or poppy seeds before baking.

FROM THE BACK: *Baking Powder Parkerhouse Rolls (page 50); Quick Cheese Crescents (page 51); White Rolls in three different shapes.*

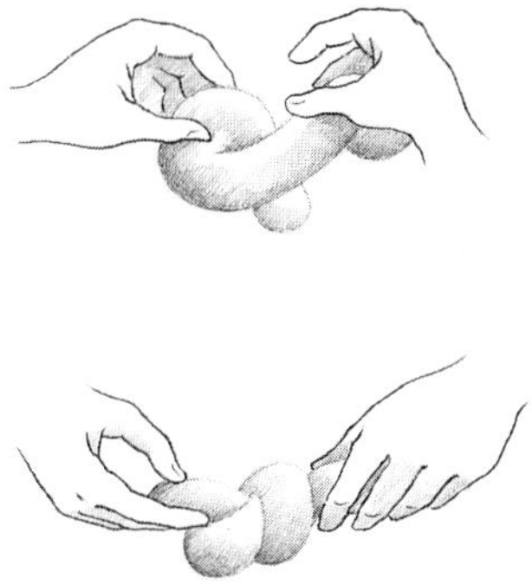

Knots
Tie 30 cm-long sausages of dough into loose knots.

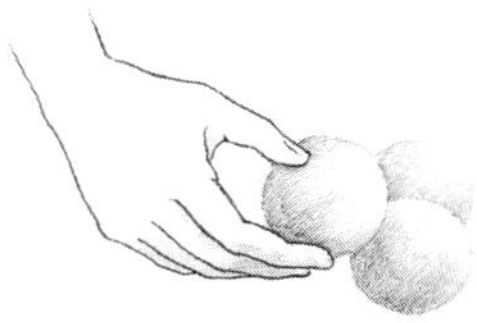

Clover Leaf Rolls
Pinch off pieces of dough, divide into three and form into small balls. Push together to join. May also be dropped into muffin tins.

Cottage Rolls
Pinch off pieces of dough and divide each piece into two thirds and one third. Roll the larger pieces into rounds, place on oiled tray and brush with milk, then roll the smaller pieces into balls and place on top. Dip your finger into flour and push right through the two balls.

Bridge Rolls
Shape dough into small sausages and place close together on tray. Before baking, sift flour over the tops. Break apart once baked.

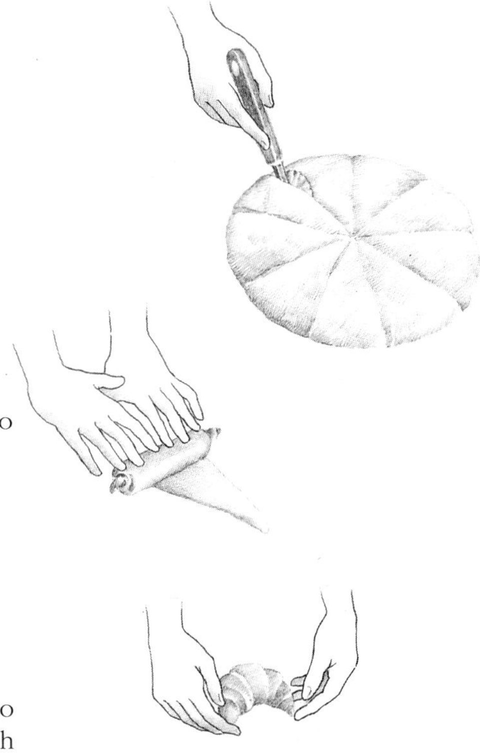

Crescents
Roll a piece of dough into a circle and cut into triangles. Roll up from long end and twist into crescent shapes.

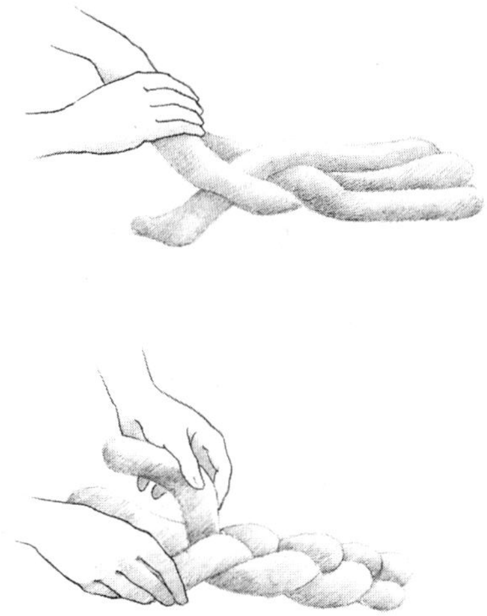

Plaits
Pinch off pieces and divide each into three. Roll into 20 cm-long sausages. Plait. Brush with milk and sprinkle with sesame seeds before baking.

VARIATION
Rosemary Rolls
For a different flavour, add a large sprig of finely chopped rosemary needles to the flour, and before baking brush tops of rolls with milk and sprinkle with crushed dried rosemary.

Croissants

10 ml sugar
50 ml warm water
15 ml dried yeast
125 ml milk
125 ml water
1 egg, separated
800 ml cake flour
5 ml salt
200 g butter
egg white, or an extra yolk beaten with 5 ml water

Stir sugar into 50 ml water, sprinkle in yeast, cover and leave to froth. Scald milk with water, then cool to lukewarm. Beat egg yolk in a small bowl or jug, stir in cooled milk-water. Stir yeast and add. Sift 200 ml of the flour with the salt and add. Beat to combine, using a wooden spoon, and then give a quick whisk with an egg beater to smooth out lumps. Sift remaining 600 ml flour into a bowl and, using two knives, or your fingertips, cut or rub in butter until particles are the size of peas. Pour liquid mixture into a well in the centre, and mix lightly with a wooden spoon until flour is thoroughly moistened and sticky. Push together with a spatula, then cover with a damp cloth. Leave to rise in a warm place until doubled – about 1¼ hours, then refrigerate, covered, until very well chilled, 1½-2 hours.

Turn onto floured board and knead very lightly with floured fingertips for a few minutes, until smooth. Cut dough into three and, using a floured rolling pin, roll each into a 25-30 cm-diameter circle. Cut into six or eight triangles. Start at the wide outer edge and roll each wedge inwards. Place, with points facing down, on oiled baking trays. Allow plenty of room for rising and spreading. Twist slightly into crescent shapes, cover loosely with lightly oiled plastic wrap and leave to rise in a warm place until doubled, about 45 minutes. The tops may be brushed with reserved egg white, but egg-wash gives a better, golden colour. Bake just above centre of oven at 220 °C for 15 minutes. Serve hot, with butter or jam.

Makes 18-24

VARIATIONS

Chocolate croissants

After cutting the triangle of dough, place two squares of dark chocolate, spaced slightly apart, in the centre, then carefully roll up as usual.

Wholewheat croissants

Make as above, except for the following alterations: Use 100 ml warm water instead of 50 ml, and 250 ml cake flour and 500 ml wholewheat flour. Sift the cake flour with the salt and add to the milk-water mixture. Whisk as before. Place wholewheat flour into a bowl and rub or cut in butter. Then proceed with the mixing and chilling as above. After cutting and shaping, the dough will need a slightly longer proving period until croissants have doubled in volume. Brush with egg-wash and bake as for white croissants.

Muffin Tin Wholewheat Rolls

A basic wholewheat batter is used for these wholesome, quickly-made muffin-shaped 'rolls'.

500-550 ml warm water
pinch sugar
10 ml dried yeast
750 ml wholewheat flour
250 ml white bread flour
125-250 ml seedless raisins (optional)
100 ml rolled oats
5 ml salt
25 ml oil
25 ml honey or half honey, half molasses
125 ml sunflower seeds
extra sunflower or sesame seeds or crushed wheat

Mix 250 ml of the water with a pinch sugar, sprinkle in yeast, cover and leave to froth. Mix remaining ingredients in large bowl. Stir frothy yeast and pour into well in centre of dry ingredients. Mix, and then slowly stir in remaining 300 ml warm water or just enough to make a thick, moist dough. Spoon into large, oiled muffin tins – they should be filled just over halfway with batter. Top with extra sunflower or sesame seeds, or crushed wheat, pressing in lightly. Cover tin lightly with oiled plastic wrap and leave in a warm place until batter rises, slightly humped, to just over the tops of the tins – 50-60 minutes. Bake just above centre of oven at 200 °C for about 25 minutes until browned and firm. Stand a few minutes and then run a knife round the edges to loosen. Cool on wire rack, and eat freshly baked.

Makes 14-16 large rolls

Baking Powder Parkerhouse Rolls

Although baking powder rolls are not as light as yeast rolls, they are useful when time is short, and delicious served freshly baked. The dough may be shaped into round balls, plaits, finger rolls or crescents, but the Parkerhouse version is particularly crusty and good.

500 ml cake flour
2 ml salt
20 ml baking powder
10 ml sugar
100 ml milk
100 ml water
20 ml butter
extra soft butter, milk and poppy seeds

Sift flour, salt and baking powder. Add sugar. Gently heat milk, water and butter together, just until butter has melted. Add to dry ingredients. Mix quickly to a soft dough, pat out 12 mm thick on floured board, and cut into rounds, using an 8 cm cutter. Make a dent down the centre of each, using the back of a knife. Spread with a little soft butter, and then fold one half over the other. Brush with milk and sprinkle with poppy seeds. Place on oiled baking tray, cover with a cloth and stand for 5 minutes, then bake just above centre of oven at 220 °C for 15-20 minutes, depending on size of rolls.

Makes about 10

Feta Cheese and Garlic Rolls

Beautiful little parcels, with a surprise in the middle. It may be gently re-heated if made ahead.

about 350 ml warm water
5 ml sugar
10 ml dried yeast
4 x 250 ml cake flour
5 ml salt
20 ml melted butter
200 g feta cheese
10 ml dried origanum
4 cloves garlic, crushed
beaten egg and milled black pepper

Pour 125 ml of the water into a mug. Stir in sugar, sprinkle in yeast, cover and leave to froth. Sift flour with salt. Stir risen yeast quickly and pour into well in centre of flour. Mix, then add remaining 225 ml water or enough to make a workable dough. Turn onto floured board and knead for 10 minutes until creamy white and smooth. Shape into a ball, brush a bowl with oil, turn dough round in bowl to coat, cover and leave to rise for 1¼ hours or until doubled.

Punch down, cover and rest 5 minutes. Roll out thinly on floured surface. Spread with butter and cut into 16 squares. Cut feta into 16 cubes and toss with origanum and garlic until coated. Place one cube in centre of each square of dough, fold corners to the centre and pinch points tightly to seal. Place parcels on oiled baking trays and cover loosely with oiled plastic wrap. Leave until well risen, about 1 hour. Brush with egg, and grind black pepper over the tops. Bake just above centre of oven at 220 °C for 15 minutes. Serve hot.
Makes 16

HINT

If bread dough does not rise, it is usually that the liquid added was either too hot or too cold. Yeast is 'tougher' than one thinks – the liquid should be warmer than lukewarm.

Slab Rusks (page 53); Wholewheat Rusks (page 52).

Quick Cheese Crescents

750 ml cake flour
15 ml baking powder
5 ml salt
5 ml dry mustard
5 ml sugar
30 ml butter
200 ml finely grated, strong Cheddar cheese
150 ml milk
150 ml water

TOPPING
melted butter
50 ml grated Cheddar cheese
or
15 ml grated Parmesan cheese
paprika

Sift flour, baking powder, salt and mustard. Add sugar and rub in butter. Mix in the cheese. Mix milk with water and add, mixing quickly and lightly to a soft but rollable dough. Divide into two, and roll out thinly on a lightly floured board into two 30 cm-diameter circles. Cut each circle across into eight triangles. Roll up each triangle from the long side towards the point. Curve slightly into horseshoe shapes and place on floured baking trays. Bake just above centre of oven at 200 °C for 15 minutes. Remove from oven and brush with melted butter, then sprinkle with Cheddar or Parmesan cheese, and dust with paprika. Return to oven and bake for 5 minutes.
Makes 16

PITA BREADS

Much experimenting has resulted in what are, to my mind, quite the best of home-made pitas. The shaping is quite different from that of ordinary bread rolls, they rise in the oven like fat little cushions, and form perfect pockets for stuffing. A high baking temperature is important, and to ensure the formation of pockets, the dough should not be creased when rolling, or pinched when turned over just prior to baking.

10 ml sugar
300 ml warm water
10 ml dried yeast
4 x 250 ml cake flour
5 ml salt
30 ml oil

Stir sugar into water. Sprinkle in yeast, cover and leave to froth. Sift flour and salt into large bowl. Add oil. Stir bubbly yeast and pour into well in centre of dry ingredients. Combine using a wooden spoon, and then mix to a dough with your hands, adding about 40 ml extra water, or enough to make a kneadable dough. Turn onto lightly floured board and knead well for 10 minutes until mixture forms a pliable ball. Return to bowl, brush top of dough with oil, cover and leave to rise for about 1 hour or until doubled in volume.

Punch down and pinch off 10 equal pieces. Roll these into balls, let it rest for 5 minutes, and then, using a rolling pin, roll into thin ovals. Place on ungreased baking trays dusted with cake flour. Leave to prove, uncovered, for about 30 minutes, until puffy and doubled in thickness. Turn over carefully and sift a little flour over the tops. Bake, one tray at a time, just above centre of oven at 240 °C for 7 minutes. Remove and wrap in a cloth to soften. Cut a small slice off the edge and press the sides gently to open out the pockets.

Makes 10

VARIATION

Wholewheat pitas

Use 500 ml white bread flour and 500 ml wholewheat flour. Sift white flour with salt, add wholewheat flour, then proceed as for white pitas. A little extra water may be necessary, but the rising and proving times are about the same.

Pita Breads form perfect pockets for stuffing with cheese, cold meats or salad.

WHOLEWHEAT RUSKS

Wholesome rusks, delicious for dunking.

1 kg wholewheat flour
500 ml white bread flour
250 ml sugar
5 ml salt
10 ml baking powder
5 ml bicarbonate of soda
5 ml cream of tartar
250 g butter, melted
200 ml seedless raisins
500 ml buttermilk
2 eggs
200 ml oil

In a large bowl mix flours, sugar, salt, baking powder, bicarbonate of soda and cream of tartar. Stir in butter and raisins. Beat buttermilk, eggs and oil. Stir into dry mixture, knead into a dough, and roll into balls about twice the size of a golf ball. Pack closely into two base-lined and oiled 23 x 8 x 7 cm loaf tins. Bake at 180 °C for 1 hour. Turn out and leave until cool enough to handle, then break apart, nick in half, and then carefully break again – use a knife to help, but rusks should always be broken, never sliced. Arrange on flat baking trays and dry out in a low oven (120-140 °C). They taste even better if allowed to toast slightly.

Makes about 72

All-Bran Buttermilk Rusks

Bran and raisins add flavour and texture to the popular dunking rusk.

500 g self-raising flour
5 ml salt
5 ml baking powder
125 ml sugar
500 ml All-Bran flakes
100 ml seedless raisins
125 g butter, melted
1 egg
250 ml buttermilk
50 ml oil

Sift flour, salt and baking powder. Add sugar, All-Bran and raisins. Mix in butter. Beat egg, buttermilk and oil together and add all at once to flour mixture. Mix to soft dough, then knead well until raisins are incorporated and dough forms a ball, leaving sides of mixing bowl clean. Pinch off pieces and roll into 16 balls. Place close together in an oiled and base-lined 26 x 9 x 7 cm loaf tin and bake at 180 °C for 1 hour. When browned, after about 40 minutes, cover with greaseproof paper. When done, turn out and leave until cool. With a sharp knife, nick tops and bottoms and carefully break into two. Place on baking trays and dry out in very low oven or warming drawer until crisp.
Makes 32

Aniseed Milk Rusks

Light, white rusks which rise like cumulus clouds.

250 ml milk
125 ml water
125 g butter
125 ml sugar
25 ml oil
1 egg, beaten
5 ml brown vinegar
1 kg self-raising flour
5 ml cream of tartar
5 ml salt
5 ml aniseed

Put milk, water, butter and sugar into a saucepan and heat gently while stirring, just until sugar has dissolved and butter has melted. Do not overheat. Remove from stove and add oil, egg and vinegar. Sift flour, cream of tartar and salt. Stir in the warm milk mixture and mix to a dough, adding a dash of water if necessary. Add aniseed and knead very well to form a smooth and pliable dough. Shape into balls, about twice the size of a golf ball, and pack closely together into one large or two small oiled and base-lined loaf tins.

Bake for 15 minutes at 200 °C, then at 180 °C for a further 45-60 minutes, depending on size of tin used. Place a sheet of greaseproof paper over the top when sufficiently browned. When done, turn out, break apart and then nick and break each ball into three or four long rusks. Arrange on baking trays and dry out at 100 °C.
Makes 36

Buttermilk Rusks

These can also be enjoyed as a delicious type of scone: turn the just-baked bun-loaf out, break apart and serve hot with butter and honey.

1,5 kg self-raising flour
10 ml salt
250 ml sugar
375 g butter
500 ml buttermilk
3 eggs

Mix flour, salt and sugar in a large mixing bowl. Rub in the butter (if in a hurry, this may be melted instead). Mix well. Beat buttermilk with eggs and add. Knead well – the more you knead, the higher they'll rise. If the dough seems a little dry, rinse the buttermilk carton with a little water and add to the mixture to make a medium-soft but never slippery dough. Continue kneading until the dough forms a ball and leaves the sides of the bowl clean, then roll into balls about twice the size of golf balls and pack closely into two base-lined, oiled and floured 26 x 9 x 7 cm loaf tins. Bake at 200 °C for 30 minutes, then reduce heat to 180 °C and bake for a further 30 minutes. Turn out and break apart and then, with the help of a knife, break into rusks. Arrange in single layers on baking trays and dry out in 120 °C oven or in warming drawer.
Makes 84-96

Slab Rusks

Definitely the easiest rusks to make – the dough is simply patted out flat into a large Swiss roll tin, cut into fingers and baked. The following recipe illustrates how white, brown, or wholewheat flour may be used with equally good results.

4 x 250 ml white bread flour
5 ml salt
10 ml cream of tartar
5 ml bicarbonate of soda
125 ml sugar
125 g butter
1 egg
250 ml buttermilk

Sift flour, salt, cream of tartar and bicarbonate of soda. Mix in sugar. Rub in butter with fingertips until finely crumbled. Beat egg with buttermilk, add to flour mixture and combine, first with a wooden spoon and then with the hands, until all the flour is gathered up and mixture forms a soft ball. Pat out into an oiled 33 x 20 cm Swiss roll tin with fairly high sides. Flour hands lightly if necessary and press out evenly, spreading right into the corners. Slice into 11 strips across and 3 strips down, making 33 fingers. Bake just above centre of oven at 200 °C for 30 minutes. Cut through again, then remove and arrange on baking trays. Dry out in warming drawer or in a 120 °C oven.
Makes 33

VARIATION
Wholewheat or brown rusks
Sift 500 ml white bread flour, salt, cream of tartar and bicarbonate of soda. Mix in 500 ml wholewheat or brown bread flour, then proceed as above.

QUICK BREADS

Maize Meal Bread

Also known as American cornbread. Baked in a square tin, cut into squares and served while hot, it is popular with fried chicken, at braais or brunches, or served with jam and butter for tea.

350 ml cake flour or white bread flour
5 ml salt
20 ml baking powder
10 ml castor sugar
300 ml fine maize meal
1 egg
300 ml milk
50 ml oil

Sift flour with salt, baking powder, sugar and maize meal. Whisk together egg, milk and oil. Pour all at once into a well in centre of dry ingredients and mix lightly and quickly, as for muffins. Pour into oiled 21 x 21 cm baking tin, spreading evenly and lightly with a spatula. Bake just above centre of oven at 220 °C for 20 minutes until golden brown and well risen. Cut into 16 squares and cool slightly before removing.
Makes 16 squares

Herbed Buttermilk Bread

A wonderfully quick loaf with a tantalizing aroma.

500 g self-raising flour
5 ml dried origanum
5 ml dried thyme
5 ml salt
5 ml sugar
100 ml finely chopped parsley
2 cloves garlic, crushed
100 ml chopped spring onions
500 ml buttermilk
50 ml water
grated Parmesan cheese and sesame seeds

Beer Bread; Feta Cheese and Garlic Rolls (page 51); Maize Meal Bread; Irish Soda Bread (page 56).

Mix together the flour, dried herbs, salt, sugar, parsley, garlic and onions. Stir in the buttermilk. Rinse the carton with the water and add, mixing well to a sticky dough. Spoon into an oiled and floured 23 x 8 x 7 cm loaf tin. Smooth the top, and then sprinkle with cheese and sesame seeds. Bake at 180 °C for 1 hour. Run a knife round the sides and turn out onto a wire rack. Serve freshly baked, with butter.
Makes 1 loaf

Savoury Cheese Soda Bread

The unusual combination of onion, carrot, herbs and cheese makes an aromatic, golden-brown loaf – a marvellous variation on the Irish soda bread theme. Serve very fresh, broken into triangles.

250 ml white bread flour
2 ml salt
2 ml bicarbonate of soda
2 ml cream of tartar
250 ml brown bread flour
15 ml butter
1 medium onion, coarsely grated
250 ml coarsely grated carrot
2 ml mixed dried herbs
50 ml chopped parsley
100 ml finely grated Cheddar cheese
about 200 ml buttermilk
milk and extra cheese or sesame seeds

Sift white bread flour, salt, bicarbonate of soda and cream of tartar. Mix in brown flour and rub in butter. Mix in onion, carrot, herbs, parsley and cheese. Add just enough buttermilk to form a soft dough. Mix lightly and then pat and toss mixture together to shape into a round. Place on floured baking tray and, using the back of a knife, score deeply into 8 triangles. Brush with milk and sprinkle either with extra cheese or sesame seeds. Bake on middle shelf of oven at 200 °C for 30 minutes. Transfer to wire rack, but serve very fresh, broken into triangles.
Makes 1 round loaf

Baking Powder Bread

A useful recipe when you need a loaf and the bread tin is empty.

4 x 250 ml white bread flour
20 ml baking powder
5 ml salt
10 ml sugar
50 ml butter
175 ml milk
175 ml water

Sift flour, baking powder and salt. Add sugar and rub in butter until finely crumbled. Mix milk and water and add, mixing quickly to a soft dough. You might have to add about 10 ml extra water. Do not knead, but pat it about until it holds together. Pat out flat into a rectangle and roll up like a Swiss roll. Place, join side down, in oiled 20 x 9 x 7 cm loaf tin. Brush with milk and bake towards the top of the oven at 220 °C for 45 minutes until golden brown. Turn out onto wire rack and cool before slicing.
Makes 1 loaf

Beer Bread

One of the quickest of breads, using the minimum of ingredients. For a different flavour, add chopped fresh herbs, crushed garlic, or cheese.

750 ml self-raising flour
250 ml wholewheat flour
2 ml salt
10 ml sugar
75 ml finely chopped parsley
1 x 340 ml bottle beer (unchilled)
sesame seeds

Mix dry ingredients, including parsley. Stir in beer, and mix to a tacky, springy dough. Turn into oiled and base-lined 20 x 9 x 7 cm loaf tin, level and sprinkle with sesame seeds. Bake at 180 °C for 1 hour 10 minutes, turn out onto wire rack, remove paper and cool. This loaf will not be browned when done, but rises well and has a crisp, humped crust. Any leftovers are good toasted.
Makes 1 loaf

Cheese, Onion and Nut Bread

Flecked with cheese and nuts, laced with onion and garlic, this is a super, fairly dense savoury loaf which takes only a few minutes from mixing bowl to oven.

750 ml self-raising flour
100 ml untoasted wheat germ
5 ml salt
5 ml sugar
3 cloves garlic, crushed
1 medium onion, coarsely grated
250 ml finely grated Cheddar cheese
125 ml finely chopped toasted walnuts or pecan nuts
250 ml buttermilk
125 ml water
paprika

Mix flour, wheat germ, salt, sugar, garlic, onion, cheese and nuts. Stir in buttermilk and water and mix to a thick and sticky batter. Turn into an oiled 23 x 8 x 7 cm loaf tin and level top with a spatula. Sprinkle with paprika and bake on middle shelf of oven at 180 °C for 1 hour. Turn out and cool on wire rack.
Makes 1 medium loaf

Irish Soda Bread

This bread does not have that overt taste of bicarb, and is a good standby when you need a small loaf. Quantities are easily doubled to make one large or two small rounds.

250 ml white bread flour
250 ml cake flour
2 ml salt
2 ml bicarbonate of soda
2 ml cream of tartar
15 ml butter
225-250 ml buttermilk
beaten egg

Sift flours with salt, bicarbonate of soda and cream of tartar. Rub in butter. Add 225 ml buttermilk all at once and mix quickly to make a soft dough, adding the extra 25 ml only if further moistening is necessary. Turn onto floured board and shape by patting into a 14 cm-diameter cake. Place on floured baking tray and score top deeply into quarters, using the back of a knife. Brush with beaten egg and bake on middle shelf of oven at 200 °C for 30 minutes. Serve freshly baked.
Makes 1 loaf

Plain Baking Powder Cob

Makes one small, crusty cob – a most useful quick-bread, and delicious served freshly baked.

375 ml cake flour
2 ml salt
20 ml baking powder
250 ml wholewheat flour
200 ml milk
1 egg
extra flour or milk and poppy seeds

Sift cake flour, salt and baking powder. Add wholewheat flour. Beat milk with egg and add. Mix to a dough, and knead lightly until it holds together. Pat into a 14 cm-diameter cake and place on floured baking tray. Make 3 diagonal slashes across the top, and either sift over a little flour, or brush with milk and sprinkle with poppy seeds. Bake just above centre of oven at 220 °C for 20-25 minutes. Transfer to wire rack and break into chunks to serve.
Makes 1 small loaf

Buttermilk Scone Bread

Serve this delicious, quickly-made bread broken into chunks, with butter and marmalade for a leisurely Sunday breakfast.

4 x 250 ml self-raising flour
5 ml salt
15 ml sugar
30 ml butter
about 425 ml buttermilk
milk, sesame and poppy seeds

Sift flour with salt. Add sugar and rub in butter. Make a well in the centre and pour in enough buttermilk to make a soft dough. Turn out onto floured board and knead very lightly while patting out to a 20 cm round, rather like a giant scone. Place on oiled baking tray and cut a fairly deep cross on the top. Brush each quarter with milk and then sprinkle alternate quarters with sesame and poppy seeds. Bake on middle shelf of oven at 220 °C for 10 minutes, then reduce heat to 180 °C and bake for 30 minutes more.
Makes 1 round loaf

HINT
● *Wholewheat and white flours can often be interchanged; however wholewheat flour will need more liquid.*

Baby Marrow Tea Loaf

A large, spicy loaf that is delicious served sliced and buttered.

3 eggs
250 ml oil
250 ml sugar
5 ml vanilla essence
300 g baby marrows
500 ml cake flour (half brown bread flour may be used)
5 ml bicarbonate of soda
5 ml baking powder
2 ml salt
5 ml ground cinnamon
5 ml ground mixed spice
125-250 ml chopped pecan nuts or walnuts

Beat eggs, oil, sugar and vanilla together until light. Trim, pare and coarsely grate raw baby marrows – you should have 500 ml – and stir in. Sift dry ingredients together and add. Finally stir in nuts. Combine thoroughly and turn into oiled, base-lined and floured 26 x 9 x 7 cm loaf tin. Bake at 180 °C on middle shelf of oven for 1 hour to 1 hour 10 minutes. Cool for 5 minutes, then turn out onto wire rack, remove paper and cool completely.
Makes 1 loaf

Cheese, Onion and Nut Bread; Irish Soda Bread.

Brown Fruit Loaf

250 g fruit cake mix
250 ml light brown sugar
250 ml water
50 ml oil
2 ml grated nutmeg
5 ml ground cinnamon
2 ml ground ginger
2 ml salt
100 ml chopped walnuts, pecan or Brazil nuts
125 ml natural drinking yoghurt
1 egg
5 ml bicarbonate of soda
500 ml brown bread flour
5 ml baking powder
5 ml vanilla essence

Put cake mixture, sugar, water, oil, spices and salt into a saucepan, bring to the boil and simmer for 5 minutes. Cool thoroughly. Add nuts. Beat yoghurt, egg and bicarbonate of soda together, and add to fruit mixture alternately with flour. Finally add baking powder and vanilla. Spoon into an oiled and floured 20 x 9 x 7 cm loaf tin and smooth top with the back of a spoon dipped into hot water. Bake at 160 °C for about 45 minutes or until skewer comes out clean. Turn out and cool on wire rack.
Makes 1 loaf

Coffee-glazed Nutmeg Loaf

Topped with flavoured glacé icing and attractively decorated, this enticing, spicy loaf looks just as good as it tastes.

500 ml cake flour
5 ml baking powder
10 ml grated nutmeg
1 ml salt
250 ml light brown sugar
125 g soft butter
200 ml buttermilk
1 egg
5 ml bicarbonate of soda
125 ml chopped Brazil nuts, lightly toasted
2 ml vanilla essence

GLAZE
125 ml sifted icing sugar
5 ml instant coffee granules
10-15 ml water
blanched almonds and cherries to decorate

Sift flour, baking powder, nutmeg and salt. Add sugar, then rub in butter until mixture is like fine breadcrumbs. (A hand-held electric beater is ideal.) Beat buttermilk with egg and bicarbonate of soda. Stir into flour mixture, then add nuts and vanilla. Mix well and turn into oiled and base-lined 20 x 9 x 7 cm loaf tin. Spread evenly, smoothing top with the back of a spoon dipped into hot water. Bake at 180 °C for 1 hour. Turn out onto wire rack, remove paper and cool. Turn right side up to glaze.

For the glaze, mix icing sugar, coffee and enough water to make a mixture that will just pour. Glaze top of loaf, allowing it to run down the sides. When set, decorate with almond 'flowers' centred with cherries. Serve sliced, with or without butter.
Makes 1 loaf

Fruit and Carrot Loaf

This budget recipe makes two medium-sized, deliciously moist loaves. Serve sliced and buttered.

250 g fruit cake mix
600 ml water
500 ml light brown sugar
500 ml coarsely grated carrots (firmly packed for measuring)
30 ml butter
10 ml ground mixed spice
500 ml cake flour
10 ml bicarbonate of soda
10 ml baking powder
1 ml salt
500 ml wholewheat flour
250 ml chopped walnuts or pecan nuts (optional)

Place fruit, water, sugar, carrots, butter and spice in a wide-based saucepan, bring to the boil, cover and simmer for 10 minutes. Cool completely. Sift cake flour with bicarbonate of soda, baking powder and salt and stir into cooled mixture. Mix in wholewheat flour – the batter will be soft. Add nuts, if using. Turn into two oiled and base-lined, or non-stick, 20 x 9 x 7 cm loaf tins, and bake at 160 °C for 1 hour. Test with a skewer, and if done, remove from oven and allow to stand for 5 minutes before inverting onto wire rack to cool.
Makes 2 loaves

Date Loaf

A simple, economical recipe.

250 g pitted dates, finely chopped
25 ml butter
250 ml light brown sugar
2 ml bicarbonate of soda
250 ml boiling water
500 ml white bread flour (half brown bread flour may be used)
1 ml salt
5 ml baking powder
2 ml vanilla essence
125 ml chopped walnuts (optional)

Put dates into a bowl with butter and sugar. Sprinkle with bicarbonate of soda and pour boiling water over. Leave to cool, stirring occasionally. Sift flour, salt and baking powder. Add cooled date mixture. Add vanilla and nuts and mix well. Pour into an oiled and base-lined 20 x 9 x 7 cm loaf tin. Level top with the back of a spoon dipped into hot water and bake at 160 °C in the centre of the oven for 1 hour. Turn out onto wire rack, remove paper and cool.
Makes 1 loaf

HINT
- *When measuring honey or syrup, use a measure that has been oiled, or used to measure oil.*

Nutty Dark Gingerbread

Satisfying and pleasantly spicy. Serve sliced and buttered.

250 ml brown sugar
125 g butter
25 ml syrup or honey
25 ml molasses
50 ml milk
50 ml water
250 ml brown bread flour
250 ml white bread flour
2 ml salt
2 ml grated nutmeg
15 ml ground ginger
7 ml baking powder
2 ml bicarbonate of soda
125 ml chopped walnuts or pecan nuts
1 egg, beaten

Heat the sugar, butter, syrup or honey, molasses, milk and water gently. Mix remaining ingredients, except egg. Pour the hot, melted ingredients into dry ingredients and mix well. Stir in egg. The mixture should be soft. Pour into oiled and floured 20 x 9 x 7 cm loaf tin and bake at 180 °C for about 45 minutes.
Makes 1 loaf

Lekach

A version of the traditional honey cake, this is a large, spicy loaf with coffee to provide the rich brown colour, and a scattering of brandy-soaked fruit. After baking, it may be topped with glacé icing and studded with blanched almonds. Serve sliced and buttered.

250 ml fruit cake mix, including some glacé cherries
2 large knobs preserved ginger, chopped
25 ml brandy
750 ml cake flour
15 ml baking powder
2 ml bicarbonate of soda
2 ml salt
15 ml ground ginger
5 ml ground cinnamon
large pinch ground cloves
250 ml light brown sugar
2 eggs
125 ml golden honey
15 ml instant coffee granules
250 ml water
125 ml oil

Place the fruit mix and ginger in small bowl. Add the brandy, cover and leave to stand for at least 1 hour. Sift the flour, baking powder, bicarbonate of soda, salt and spices together, then add the sugar. Beat the eggs until light, then beat in the honey, the coffee dissolved in the water, and the oil. Add to flour mixture and mix well until thoroughly combined. Fold in the fruit and turn into a base-lined and oiled 26 x 9 x 7 cm loaf tin. Bake the lekach on the middle shelf of the oven at 180 °C for 1 hour 15 minutes. Test with a skewer, then leave to stand a few minutes before turning out onto a wire rack to cool.
Makes 1 very large loaf

HINT
- *Lightly toasting nuts before use brings out the flavour. Chop nuts, then spread them out on baking trays and place in moderate oven until lightly browned.*

FROM LEFT TO RIGHT: *Date Loaf; All-Bran Fruit Loaf; Fruit and Carrot Loaf.*

All-Bran Fruit Loaf

250 ml All-Bran flakes
200 ml light brown sugar
250 ml fruit cake mix
250 ml milk
60 ml oil
375 ml cake flour
15 ml baking powder
2 ml salt
5 ml ground mixed spice
100 ml finely chopped pecan nuts (optional)
5 ml vanilla essence

Place the All-Bran, sugar, fruit, milk and oil in large mixing bowl. Stir until combined and then leave to stand for 30 minutes. Sift the flour, baking powder, salt and spice. Add to the fruit mixture, together with nuts, if using, and vanilla. Mix well, using a wooden spoon. Turn into an oiled and base-lined 20 x 9 x 7 cm loaf tin and bake on the middle shelf of the oven at 180 °C for 1 hour, then test with a skewer. If done, leave to stand for a few minutes before turning out onto wire rack to cool. Serve sliced and lightly buttered.
Makes 1 loaf

Chocolate, Carrot and Ginger Loaf

This is quite different from the regular carrot loaf; it is large, dark and economical, with an unusual combination of ingredients. Serve sliced and buttered, rather than iced.

250 ml cake flour
50 ml cocoa powder
5 ml ground mixed spice
5 ml bicarbonate of soda
5 ml baking powder
1 ml salt
250 ml wholewheat flour
200 ml seedless raisins
3 knobs preserved ginger, chopped
125 ml desiccated coconut
2 eggs*
250 ml light brown sugar
125 ml oil
500 ml coarsely grated carrots
5 ml vanilla essence

Sift cake flour, cocoa, spice, bicarbonate of soda, baking powder and salt. Add wholewheat flour, raisins, ginger and coconut. Beat eggs, sugar and oil. Add to flour mixture, and when combined, stir in carrots and vanilla. Mix to a fairly stiff, sticky batter. Turn into oiled and base-lined 23 x 8 x 7 cm loaf tin, smooth the top with the back of a spoon dipped into hot water, and bake on the middle shelf of the oven at 180 °C for about 1 hour 10 minutes – test with a skewer. Stand a few minutes before turning out onto wire rack to cool.
Makes 1 loaf

* It is important to use extra large or jumbo eggs, or batter will be too stiff.

Tea Fruit Loaf

This is just one good version of the ever popular cold tea fruit loaf, which rises beautifully without humping.

500 g fruit cake mix
2 tea bags (Rooibos or other)
500 ml boiling water
25 ml oil
2 eggs, lightly beaten
375 ml light brown sugar
4 x 250 ml self-raising flour
2 ml salt
5 ml ground cinnamon
5 ml ground mixed spice
5 ml baking powder
5 ml vanilla essence

Put fruit and tea bags into bowl. Pour boiling water over, stir and leave overnight. Next day turn mixture into large mixing bowl, remove tea bags, and add oil, eggs and sugar, mixing well. Sift flour, salt, spices and baking powder. Add to fruit mixture, mix well, and stir in vanilla. Turn mixture, which will be thick and sticky, into two oiled and base-lined 20 x 9 x 7 cm loaf tins. Level tops with the back of a spoon dipped into hot water. Bake on middle shelf of oven at 180 °C for 1-1¼ hours – test with a skewer to make sure they are cooked through. Turn out onto wire rack, remove paper and leave to cool. Serve sliced and buttered.
Makes 2 loaves

Coconut Yoghurt Loaf

This large, moist loaf, is also known as Tub Loaf, as all the measuring is conveniently done in the yoghurt tub.

1 x 175 ml tub natural Bulgarian yoghurt
1 tub sugar
1 tub oil
3 eggs
5 ml vanilla essence
3 tubs self-raising flour
2 tubs desiccated coconut

Whisk together the yoghurt, sugar, oil, eggs and vanilla until thick and creamy. Add flour, one tub at a time, mixing well. Add coconut and mix to a very soft batter. Pour into oiled and base-lined 26 x 9 x 7 cm loaf tin and bake on middle shelf of oven at 160 °C for 1¼ hours. Stand a few minutes before turning out onto wire rack to cool.
Makes 1 loaf

Glazed Lemon Loaf

Light, lovely and lemony.

125 g soft butter
200 ml castor sugar
10 ml finely grated lemon rind
500 ml white bread flour plus 10 ml extra
10 ml baking powder
1 ml salt
100 ml finely chopped mixed peel
2 eggs
250 ml milk
2 ml vanilla essence

GLAZE
50 ml castor sugar
50 ml fresh lemon juice

Cream butter, sugar and lemon rind until light. Sift flour, baking powder and salt. Add the mixed peel. Add eggs to creamed mixture, one at a time, adding 5 ml flour with each egg. Fold in flour mixture, and then add milk and vanilla. Whisk to make a soft batter. Pour into an oiled, base-lined 23 x 8 x 7 cm loaf tin and smooth top with the back of a spoon dipped into hot water. Bake at 180 °C for 1 hour.

Just before the end of the baking time, prepare the glaze by mixing castor sugar and lemon juice in small saucepan. Stir gently over low heat to dissolve sugar and then boil over high heat for 1 minute. Remove the baked loaf from the oven, prick the top all over with a thin skewer, and slowly drizzle lemon syrup over. Stand in tin until completely cold. To loosen, run a knife round the edges and turn out.
Makes 1 loaf

FROM THE BACK: *Coconut Yoghurt Loaf; Chocolate Carrot and Ginger Loaf; Glazed Lemon Loaf.*

One-bowl Orange Loaf

A great standby when time is at a premium – assemble the ingredients and whip up this loaf for tea in a matter of minutes.

500 ml cake flour or white bread flour
200 ml castor sugar
10 ml baking powder
1 ml salt
125 ml oil
125 ml fresh orange juice
5 ml finely grated orange rind
2 eggs
2 ml vanilla essence

GLAZE
25 ml orange juice
10 ml butter
250 ml sifted icing sugar

Sift flour, sugar, baking powder and salt into mixing bowl. Add oil, juice and rind. Using an electric beater, mix for 1 minute on medium speed. Add eggs and vanilla. Beat for 45 seconds or just until well mixed. Pour into a base-lined, oiled and floured 23 x 8 x 7 cm loaf tin and bake at 160 °C on middle shelf of oven for 1 hour. Stand 5 minutes, then turn out and cool on wire rack.

To make the glaze, heat orange juice and butter in small saucepan, add icing sugar and stir over very low heat until smooth. Pour over top of cold loaf, allowing glaze to trickle down the sides. Decorate with cherries and angelica.
Makes 1 loaf

HINT
- *Do not add too much liquid to a batter bread. If you make it too wet, the loaf will deflate in the oven. The consistency should be fairly thick and moist, like a fruit cake mixture.*

One-bowl Orange Loaf; Banana Loaf; Baby Marrow Tea Loaf (page 57).

Pumpkin, Pecan and Raisin Loaf

A spicy, caramel-coloured loaf, delicious served sliced and buttered. Be sure to use a bright orange pumpkin, and drain very well after cooking.

500 ml white bread flour
5 ml baking powder
2 ml salt
5 ml ground cinnamon
5 ml ground ginger
large pinch ground cloves
100 ml finely chopped pecan nuts
150 ml seedless raisins
100 g soft butter
250 ml light brown sugar
2 eggs
375 ml smooth pumpkin purée
5 ml bicarbonate of soda
25 ml water

Sift flour, baking powder, salt and spices. Add nuts and raisins. Cream butter and sugar. Add eggs singly, beating well. Mix in pumpkin purée, and then add flour mixture, beating until combined. Dissolve bicarbonate of soda in the water and stir into batter. Turn into oiled and base-lined 23 x 8 x 7 cm loaf tin, and bake at 180 °C for 1 hour. Stand for 5 minutes before turning out on wire rack to cool.
Makes 1 loaf

Banana Loaf

A reliable old favourite.

500 ml white or brown bread flour
10 ml baking powder
1 ml bicarbonate of soda
2 ml salt
5 ml ground cinnamon
125 g butter
250 ml sugar
2 eggs
4 large, ripe bananas, mashed
125 ml chopped walnuts
2 ml vanilla essence

Sift flour with baking powder, bicarbonate of soda, salt and cinnamon. Cream butter and sugar until light. Add eggs singly, beating well between additions and adding 5 ml of the flour mixture with each egg. Add flour mixture to creamed mixture alternately with bananas, beating well until smooth. Stir in nuts and vanilla. Pour into lightly oiled and base-lined 26 x 9 x 7 cm loaf tin. Smooth top with the back of a spoon dipped into hot water, then bake at 180 °C for 50-60 minutes. Turn out, remove paper and cool. Serve sliced and buttered.
Makes 1 loaf

Buttermilk Fruit Loaf

A large, economical and easy-to-make loaf, rather like a light, slab fruit cake. Serve sliced and buttered.

750 ml self-raising flour
5 ml ground cinnamon
2 ml grated nutmeg
2 ml salt
375 ml fruit cake mix
375 ml buttermilk
1 egg
50 ml honey
75 ml sugar
100 ml oil
cherries and blanched almonds

Sift flour, spices and salt. Mix in fruit. Whisk together buttermilk, egg, honey, sugar and oil. Add to flour mixture and combine lightly but thoroughly. Turn into a base-lined and oiled 26 x 9 x 7 cm loaf tin and level top with back of a spoon dipped into hot water. As the batter is fairly stiff, cherries and almonds may be arranged on the top. Bake on middle shelf of oven at 180 °C for 1 hour. Stand 1 minute before turning out onto wire rack to cool.
Makes 1 loaf

Surprise Loaf

Flecked with colour, this tea loaf combines two vegetables in a most unusual and delicious way. Serve sliced and buttered.

200 ml oil
250 ml sugar
2 eggs
100 ml sunflower seeds (preferably toasted)
250 ml coarsely grated carrots
250 ml peeled and coarsely grated beetroot
250 ml cake flour
2 ml salt
15 ml baking powder
5 ml ground cinnamon
2 ml ground mixed spice
250 ml wholewheat flour

Whisk oil and sugar until creamy, then add eggs and beat well. Mix in sunflower seeds, carrots and beetroot. Sift cake flour, salt, baking powder and spices, and add to creamed mixture. Fold in wholewheat flour. Turn into oiled and base-lined 26 x 9 x 7 cm loaf tin and bake at 180 °C for 1 hour. Stand 1 minute, then turn out onto wire rack to cool.
Makes 1 loaf

MUFFINS

Basic Muffins

Plain, golden muffins, equally good served with butter and cheese, honey or jam.

500 ml cake flour
15 ml baking powder
2 ml salt
50 ml sugar
60 ml oil
1 egg, beaten
125 ml milk
125 ml water

Sift flour, baking powder and salt. Add sugar. Whisk together the oil, egg, milk and water. Pour into a well in centre of dry ingredients. Mix lightly and quickly – use a wooden spoon and do not beat. Spoon into oiled muffin tins, making them two-thirds full. Bake at 200 °C for 20-25 minutes. Cool slightly before loosening with a knife and removing. Serve as soon as possible.
Makes 12

Apple, Raisin and Honey Muffins

250 ml white bread flour
5 ml ground cinnamon
1 ml grated nutmeg
small pinch ground cloves
2 ml salt
15 ml baking powder
250 ml wholewheat flour
1 egg
50 ml oil
125 ml water
125 ml milk
50 ml light brown sugar
50 ml honey
2 medium Golden Delicious apples
75 ml seedless raisins

Sift white flour, spices, salt and baking powder. Mix in wholewheat flour. Whisk together the egg, oil, water, milk, sugar and honey. Make a well in centre of dry ingredients and pour in the liquid ingredients. Add peeled and coarsely grated apples, as well as raisins. Stir lightly and quickly until just combined – do not beat. Spoon into oiled and floured muffin tins, making them three-quarters full, and bake at 200 °C for 20 minutes. Run a knife round the edges to loosen, and turn out on a wire rack to cool. Serve split and buttered.
Makes 12-14

Basic Muffins; Apple, Raisin and Honey Muffins.

Favourite Fruit Muffins

Flop-proof, nutritious, sweet and spicy muffins which rise perfectly. Split and buttered they are great for lunch-boxes. A handful of chopped nuts may be added with the sugar, if desired.

250 ml boiling water
250 ml fruit cake mix
25 ml butter
250 ml white bread flour
5 ml baking powder
5 ml bicarbonate of soda
2 ml salt
5 ml ground mixed spice
2 ml ground cinnamon
250 ml wholewheat flour
100 ml light brown sugar
2 ml vanilla essence

Pour water over fruit and butter in a bowl and let it stand for 10 minutes, stirring once to melt butter. Sift together white flour, baking powder, bicarbonate of soda, salt and spices. Add wholewheat flour and sugar. Pour fruit mixture into a well in the centre of the dry ingredients and mix together with vanilla until just combined – do not overmix. Spoon into oiled muffin tins, making them two-thirds full. Bake at 200 °C for 15-18 minutes until richly browned and firm. Run a knife round the edges to remove and turn out on a wire rack to cool. Serve freshly baked, with butter.
Makes 12-14

Processor Herb Muffins

Fragrant with herbs and made in a jiffy, these muffins are splendid served hot from the oven with a bowl of soup. The amount of herbs is approximate – there is no need to count little leaves and sprigs meticulously – let the quantities merely act as a guide. The important factor is to use fresh herbs.

4 sprigs marjoram
2 sprigs thyme
about 24 rosemary needles
8 large sage leaves
few sprigs parsley
500 ml cake flour
15 ml baking powder
2 ml salt
5 ml sugar
1 large clove garlic, chopped
2 spring onions, plus some tops, chopped
1 egg
60 ml oil
200 ml milk
grated Cheddar cheese

Strip leaves from marjoram and thyme and place in processor fitted with grinding blade together with the rosemary, sage, parsley, flour, baking powder, salt, sugar, garlic and spring onions. Process until herbs are finely chopped. Tip into mixing bowl. Beat egg with oil and milk. Pour into well in centre of flour mixture and mix very quickly to a soft batter. Pour into well-oiled muffin tins, making them about two-thirds full. Sprinkle with the cheese and bake at 200 °C for 20-25 minutes. Stand a few seconds and then run a knife round the edges to loosen. Serve hot, with butter.
Makes 12 large muffins

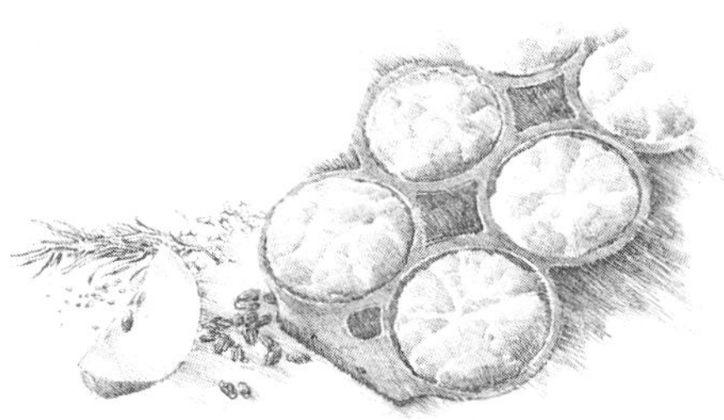

Spring Onion, Cheese and Celery Muffins

Aromatic muffins, super with soup.

500 ml self-raising flour
2 ml dry mustard
2 ml salt
60 g butter
2 large sticks table celery
4 spring onions, plus some of the tops, chopped
125 ml grated Cheddar cheese
1 egg
250 ml buttermilk
paprika

Sift flour, mustard and salt. Rub in butter until finely crumbled. Grate celery coarsely and squeeze dry with paper towels if necessary. Add to dry mixture together with onions and cheese. Beat egg with buttermilk and add. Mix quickly and spoon into oiled muffin tins, making them two-thirds full. Dust with paprika and bake at 200 °C for 20-25 minutes. Stand 1 minute before removing. Serve warm with butter.
Makes 12-14

Cottage Cheese, Green Pepper and Onion Muffins

Aromatic, savoury muffins which rise splendidly – so be sure not to overfill the tins.

1 egg
50 ml oil
125 ml smooth cottage cheese
100 ml milk
100 ml water
500 ml cake flour
15 ml baking powder
2 ml salt
60 ml finely chopped green pepper (discard all seeds and ribs)
6 spring onions, chopped
2 ml mixed dried herbs
12-16 small cubes of Gouda cheese

Beat together egg, oil, cottage cheese, milk and water in mixing bowl. Sift flour, baking powder and salt. Add to liquid mixture, stir until just combined, then add green pepper, onions, and herbs. Mix quickly and lightly. Spoon into oiled muffin tins, making them two-thirds full, and top each with a cube of Gouda. Bake on middle shelf of oven at 200 °C for 25 minutes. Run a knife round the edges to loosen, and remove.
Makes 12-16

HINT
- *If your bread or muffins won't turn out easily, let them stand for a minute or two, then run a knife around the sides and either invert or ease out.*

All-Bran Banana Muffins

Moist, brown and flavoursome.

250 ml cake flour
1 ml salt
5 ml ground cinnamon
5 ml ground mixed spice
15 ml baking powder
250 ml All-Bran flakes, coarsely crushed
100 ml sugar
60 g soft butter
3 large, ripe bananas
1 egg
125 ml milk
25 ml honey
2 ml vanilla essence
100 ml toasted sunflower seeds or 125 ml chopped pecan nuts

Sift flour, salt, spices and baking powder. Mix in cereal and sugar. Rub in butter. Mash bananas and whisk together with egg, milk, honey and vanilla. Add to flour mixture together with sunflower seeds or nuts. Mix lightly until just combined and spoon into oiled muffin tins, making them two-thirds full. Bake at 200 °C for 20 minutes. Stand a few minutes before removing.
Makes 14

Overnight Muffins

Mix these the day before, and have muffins on tap for breakfast.

250 ml wholewheat flour
250 ml white bread flour or cake flour
125 ml sugar
60 ml oil
2 ml vanilla essence
7 ml bicarbonate of soda
1 egg, beaten
1 ml salt
250 ml milk
5 ml ground cinnamon
2 ml grated nutmeg
200 ml seedless raisins
125 ml chopped walnuts or pecan nuts (optional)

Mix all the ingredients together, but mix raisins and nuts in last. Cover batter and refrigerate overnight. Spoon into oiled muffin tins, making them three-quarters full. Bake at 200 °C for 15-20 minutes, until well risen and browned.
Makes about 18

Honey Fruit Muffins

250 ml cake flour
2 ml salt
5 ml bicarbonate of soda
2 ml ground mixed spice
60 ml light brown sugar
250 ml wholewheat flour
200 ml seedless raisins
50 ml mixed peel
1 egg
60 ml oil
60 ml light honey
250 ml buttermilk

Sift cake flour, salt, bicarbonate of soda and spice. Mix in sugar, wholewheat flour, raisins and mixed peel. Whisk together egg, oil, honey and buttermilk. Add to dry ingredients and mix quickly to a lumpy batter. Spoon into oiled muffin tins, making them three-quarters full, and bake at 200 °C for 20-22 minutes. Stand for a minute before running a knife round the edges to remove.
Makes 12 large muffins

GINGER NUT MUFFINS

500 ml cake flour
15 ml baking powder
2 ml salt
10 ml ground ginger
50 ml sugar
4 knobs preserved ginger, chopped
125 ml chopped walnuts or pecan nuts
60 ml oil
1 egg, beaten
125 ml milk
125 ml water
25 ml ginger syrup

Sift dry ingredients. Add sugar, preserved ginger and nuts. Whisk together oil, egg, milk, water and syrup. Pour all at once into well in centre of dry ingredients, mix lightly and quickly, using a wooden spoon. Spoon into oiled muffin tins, making them two-thirds full. Bake at 200 °C for 20-25 minutes. Cool slightly before removing.
Makes 12

LIGHT CHOCOLATE MUFFINS

500 ml cake flour
15 ml baking powder
2 ml salt
25 ml cocoa powder
100 ml sugar
125 ml chopped walnuts or pecan nuts
60 ml oil
1 egg, beaten
125 ml milk
125 ml water
10 ml instant coffee granules

Sift dry ingredients, except coffee. Add sugar and nuts. Whisk together oil, egg, milk, water and coffee. Pour into well in centre of dry ingredients. Mix very lightly, using a wooden spoon. Spoon into oiled muffin tins, making them two-thirds full. Bake at 200 °C for 20-25 minutes. Cool slightly before removing.
Makes 12

Savoury muffins such as Cottage Cheese, Green Pepper and Onion Muffins, and Spring Onion, Cheese and Celery Muffins, go well with soup.

Carrot and Fruit Muffins; Health Muffins; Coconut Currant Muffins.

CHEESE AND HERB MUFFINS

Savoury wholewheat muffins to accompany soups or salads.

250 ml cake flour
20 ml baking powder
2 ml salt
5 ml dry mustard
250 ml wholewheat flour
5 ml dried mixed herbs
10 ml sugar
50 ml finely chopped parsley
250 ml grated Cheddar cheese
1 egg
250 ml milk
60 ml oil
extra grated cheese or sesame seeds

Sift cake flour, baking powder, salt and mustard. Mix in wholewheat flour, herbs, sugar, parsley and cheese. Beat egg with milk and oil, pour into dry mixture and mix lightly. Spoon into oiled muffin tins, making them two-thirds full, sprinkle with extra cheese or sesame seeds and bake at 200 °C for 25 minutes. Cool slightly and run a knife round the edges to remove.
Makes 12-14

CARROT AND FRUIT MUFFINS

Add a handful of sunflower seeds or chopped walnuts for crunch.

125 ml seedless raisins
50 ml chopped mixed peel
250 ml water
200-250 ml light brown sugar
250 ml coarsely grated carrots
25 ml butter
5 ml ground mixed spice
250 ml cake flour
5 ml bicarbonate of soda
5 ml baking powder
1 ml salt
250 ml wholewheat flour
125 ml desiccated coconut
2 ml vanilla essence

Place fruit, water, sugar, carrots, butter and spice in saucepan. Bring to the boil, cover and simmer gently for 10 minutes. Cool completely. Sift dry ingredients and stir into fruit mixture. Add wholewheat flour, coconut and vanilla, and nuts if using. Spoon into oiled muffin tins, making them two-thirds full. Bake at 200 °C for 18-20 minutes. Cool in tins for 1 minute before removing.
Makes 12-14

HINT
- *Wholewheat and white flours can often be interchanged; however wholewheat flour will need more liquid.*

HEALTH MUFFINS

These wholesome muffins, containing rye and wholewheat flours, will not rise quite as high as those using refined ingredients. Molasses adds colour and flavour, while raisins and sunflower seeds provide extra nutrition.

125 ml self-raising flour
2 ml salt
7 ml baking powder
5 ml ground mixed spice
100 ml castor sugar
250 ml wholewheat flour
100 ml rye flour
125 ml seedless raisins
100 ml sunflower seeds
1 egg
250 ml buttermilk
20 ml molasses
125 ml oil

Sift self-raising flour, salt, baking powder, spice and sugar. Mix in wholewheat and rye flours. Add raisins and sunflower seeds. Whisk together egg, buttermilk, molasses and oil. Add to flour mixture and mix lightly. Spoon into oiled muffin tins, making them two-thirds full, and bake at 200 °C for 25 minutes.
Makes 16

NUTTY DATE MUFFINS

250 g pitted dates, finely chopped
50 ml mixed peel
25 ml butter
250 ml boiling water
250 ml cake flour
5 ml baking powder
5 ml bicarbonate of soda
1 ml salt
5 ml ground cinnamon
1 ml grated nutmeg
pinch ground cloves
250 ml wholewheat flour
100 ml light brown sugar
100 ml chopped walnuts or pecan nuts
2 ml vanilla essence
100 ml buttermilk

Put dates, mixed peel and butter into bowl, pour boiling water over, stir to mix and then leave to cool. Sift cake flour, baking powder, bicarbonate of soda, salt and spices. Add wholewheat flour and sugar. Mix in cooled date mixture, nuts and vanilla and then quickly moisten with buttermilk. Spoon into oiled muffin tins, making them two-thirds full. Bake at 200 °C for 15-20 minutes.
Makes 12-16

COCONUT CURRANT MUFFINS

500 ml cake flour
15 ml baking powder
2 ml salt
100 ml sugar
200 ml desiccated coconut
100 ml currants
60 ml oil
1 egg, beaten
125 ml milk
125 ml water
extra desiccated coconut

Sift flour, baking powder and salt. Add sugar, coconut and currants. Whisk together the oil, egg, milk and water. Pour all at once into well in centre of dry ingredients. Mix lightly and quickly – the batter should be lumpy. Spoon into oiled muffin tins, making them two-thirds full, sprinkle tops with extra coconut and bake at 200 °C for 20-25 minutes. Cool slightly before removing.
Makes 12

CHEESE MUFFINS

Using half milk and half water makes muffins extra light, as in these golden-brown savoury muffins – delicious served hot with butter. For added flavour, strip the leaves off a few sprigs of fresh thyme and add with the cheese.

375 ml cake flour
15 ml baking powder
2 ml salt
5 ml dry mustard
250 ml finely grated, strong Cheddar cheese
5 ml sugar
75 ml milk
75 ml water
60 ml oil
1 egg
paprika and/or tiny cubes of cheese

Sift flour, baking powder, salt and mustard powder. Mix in cheese and sugar. Whisk together milk, water, oil and egg. Add to flour mixture and stir quickly until just combined – the mixture will not be smooth. Spoon into oiled muffin tins, making them two-thirds full, and sprinkle with paprika, placing a tiny cube of cheese in the middle, if using. Bake on middle shelf of oven at 200 °C for 25 minutes. Stand for a minute, then run a knife round the edges to loosen, and remove.
Makes 12

SCONES

Basic Featherlight Scones

These are the high-rise, fluffy scones to serve with jam and cream.

500 ml cake flour
20 ml baking powder
1 ml salt
25 ml sugar
60 g soft butter
50 ml milk
50 ml water
1 egg
2 ml lemon juice

GLAZE
1 egg yolk beaten with 5 ml water

Sift flour, baking powder and salt. Add sugar, then rub in butter. Beat together milk, water, egg and lemon juice. Pour into a well in the centre of the dry ingredients. Mix lightly with a fork to a soft dough, then pat out on lightly floured board. Working quickly, either cut into squares, or cut into rounds with a 6 cm cutter. Place on lightly oiled or non-stick baking tray. Glaze with egg-wash and bake towards top of oven at 220 °C for 12 minutes. Serve as fresh as possible.
Makes 10

Golden-Topped Cheese Scones

Delicious scones with a topping of cheese, butter and Marmite.

500 ml cake flour or white bread flour
20 ml baking powder
2 ml dry mustard
1 ml salt
pinch cayenne pepper
250 ml grated Cheddar cheese
50 ml oil
1 egg
50 ml milk
50 ml water

TOPPING
25 ml melted butter
125 ml grated Cheddar cheese
2 ml Marmite

Sift together flour, baking powder, mustard, salt and cayenne. Add cheese. Beat together oil, egg, milk and water. Pour into a well in centre of dry ingredients and mix lightly with a fork until dough holds together. Pat out 2 cm thick on lightly floured board, cut into rounds with 6 cm scone cutter and place on oiled baking tray.

Mash together all the ingredients for topping and place a teaspoonful on top of each scone. Bake towards the top of the oven at 220 °C for 12 minutes. Serve hot with butter.
Makes 10-12

Basic Featherlight Scones; Brown Raisin and Spice scones (page 73).

Dropped Cheese Scones

These exceptionally light and quickly-made scones require no cutting. They are delicious served hot with butter for tea or a special breakfast.

500 ml cake flour
15 ml baking powder
5 ml sugar
2 ml salt
5 ml dry mustard
125 ml grated mature Cheddar cheese
1 egg
100 ml milk
100 ml water
50 ml oil
paprika

Sift together flour, baking powder, sugar, salt and mustard. Add cheese. Beat together the egg, milk, water and oil. Make a well in the centre of the dry ingredients and pour in the liquid. Mix lightly and quickly to a soft dough, using a fork. Drop spoonfuls onto an oiled baking tray, dust the tops with paprika and bake towards the top of the oven at 220 °C for 10-12 minutes.
Makes 12

Sour Cream, Sage and Chive Scones

A delicious, savoury scone. If fresh herbs are not available, 5 ml dried mixed herbs may be substituted, but the flavour will not be the same.

500 ml self-raising flour
2 ml salt
10 ml castor sugar
125 ml sour cream
25 ml finely chopped chives
16 fresh sage leaves, finely chopped
50 ml finely chopped parsley
1 egg
50 ml water
milk and poppy seeds

Sift flour, salt and sugar. Mix in sour cream and herbs. Beat egg with water and add, mixing to a soft dough. Turn onto floured board and pat out 2 cm thick. Cut into squares, or into rounds, using a 6 cm floured cutter and being careful not to twist when cutting. Place on oiled baking tray, brush with milk and sprinkle with poppy seeds. Bake towards top of oven at 220 °C for 12 minutes. Serve hot.
Makes 8-10

Fat-Free Scones

A plain, basic scone containing neither eggs nor butter.

500 ml self-raising flour
2 ml salt
20 ml castor sugar
50 ml fat-free milk powder
150 ml water
60 ml oil

Sift flour, salt and sugar. Mix milk powder into water and beat together with oil. Add to flour and mix lightly. Pat out 2 cm thick on lightly floured board and cut, using a 6 cm cutter. Place on oiled baking tray and bake towards top of oven at 220 °C for 12 minutes. Serve hot, with butter and cheese, or jam.
Makes 10

Wholewheat Fruit Scones

Serve hot with butter and marmalade.

250 ml white bread flour
20 ml baking powder
2 ml salt
375 ml wholewheat flour
200 ml fruit cake mix
25 ml brown sugar
5 ml finely grated orange rind (optional)
1 egg
75 ml milk
75 ml water
25 ml honey
75 ml oil

TOPPING
10 ml sugar
2 ml ground cinnamon

Sift white bread flour, baking powder and salt together. Add wholewheat flour, fruit, sugar and rind. Beat egg, milk, water, honey and oil together and pour into well in centre of dry ingredients. Using a fork, mix quickly to form a soft dough. Pat out into a round on a lightly floured board, brush with egg glaze or milk, and sprinkle with topping. Using a sharp knife, cut right through into 8-10 wedges and place on oiled baking tray. Bake just above the centre of the oven at 220 °C for 15-18 minutes.
Makes 8-10 wedges

Ginger Scones

500 ml cake flour
20 ml baking powder
2 ml salt
25 ml castor sugar
5 ml ground ginger
60 g butter
3-4 large knobs preserved ginger, finely chopped
50 ml mixed peel, finely chopped
60 ml milk
60 ml water
1 egg

Sift flour, baking powder, salt, sugar and ginger. Rub in butter. Add chopped ginger and mixed peel. Beat together milk, water and egg. Add to dry ingredients and mix lightly with a fork to a soft ball. Pat out 2 cm thick on floured board – you may have to flour your hands a little – and cut into 6 cm rounds, or squares, or triangles. Place on oiled baking tray and bake towards top of oven at 220 °C for 12 minutes.
Makes about 12

NOTE
- *A dash of lemon juice added to the liquid, will lighten scones.*
- *Instead of breaking an egg just for glazing, milk may be used, but the scones will not have the same rich colour.*

Pumpkin Scones

Serve these with butter and honey. Use a bright orange pumpkin, and drain well after cooking.

60 g soft butter
125 ml light brown sugar
1 egg, lightly beaten
750 ml self-raising flour
2 ml salt
10 ml ground ginger
5 ml ground cinnamon
pinch ground cloves
125 ml seedless raisins
250 ml smooth pumpkin purée
50 ml chopped mixed peel

Cream butter and sugar. Beat in egg, adding 5 ml of the flour. Sift flour, salt and spices and add. Mix well, then add raisins, pumpkin and mixed peel. Mix to a soft dough – no liquid is required, as the puréed pumpkin should moisten the mixture sufficiently. Pat out 2 cm thick onto floured board and cut into rounds, using a floured 6 cm cutter. Place on oiled baking tray and brush tops with egg glaze. Bake just above centre of oven at 220 °C for 12 minutes.
Makes 14-16

Wholewheat Cheese Scones

250 ml white bread flour
15 ml baking powder
2 ml salt
10 ml castor sugar
5 ml dry mustard
250 ml wholewheat flour
50 ml butter
250 ml grated Cheddar cheese
1 egg
50 ml milk
50 ml water

GLAZE
1 egg yolk beaten with 5 ml water
paprika

Sift white bread flour with baking powder, salt, sugar and mustard. Add wholewheat flour, rub in butter, then add cheese. Beat egg, milk and water together and add. Mix with a fork and then lightly form into a ball, adding, if necessary, 5-10 ml water. Pat out on lightly floured board and, using a knife, cut into 9 squares. Place on oiled baking tray. Brush with egg-wash, sprinkle with paprika and bake towards top of oven at 220 °C for 12 minutes. Serve hot with butter and honey.
Makes 9

Spicy Fruit Scones

Sweet and satisfying tea-time scones, topped with cinnamon-sugar.

500 ml self-raising flour
2 ml salt
5 ml ground mixed spice
25 ml sugar
60 g soft butter
150 ml fruit cake mix
1 egg
50 ml milk
50 ml water

TOPPING
milk
5 ml sugar
2 ml ground cinnamon

Sift flour, salt and spice. Add sugar and rub in butter. Add fruit cake mix. Beat egg, milk and water. Pour into a well in centre of dry ingredients and mix lightly with a fork. When thoroughly combined, pat out on lightly floured board and cut into squares or rounds, using a 6 cm cutter. Place on oiled baking tray, brush with milk and sprinkle with sugar mixed with cinnamon. Bake just above centre of oven at 220 °C for 12 minutes.
Makes 10

NOTE
- *When using a scone cutter, be careful not to twist when you cut out the scones.*

Golden-topped Cheese Scones; Jiffy Scones; Sour Cream Sage and Chive Scones.

Jiffy Scones

These quickly-made light, white scones rise like little stuffed pillows, especially if you cut them into squares instead of rounds – remember that cutters, if twisted, will frighten the life out of scones, apart from the disadvantage of re-patting out any leftover dough. These delicious scones may be served with either sweet or savoury toppings.

500 ml self-raising flour
2 ml salt
15 ml castor sugar
1 egg
60 ml oil
buttermilk
milk or egg-wash

Sift flour, salt and sugar. Break egg into a 500 ml measuring jug. Add oil and enough buttermilk to fill the jug to the 200 ml mark. Whisk well and then add to dry ingredients. Mix quickly, using a fork, until mixture holds together, then toss into a ball with your hands. Pat out 2 cm thick on lightly floured board, and cut into desired shapes. Place on oiled baking tray, brush with milk or egg-wash, and bake just above centre of oven at 220 °C for 12 minutes.
Makes about 10

Brown Raisin and Spice Scones

Sugar and spice – and plump raisins – add a glass of sherry and its just the thing to warm up a cold and wintry afternoon.

250 ml cake flour
20 ml baking powder
2 ml salt
50 ml castor sugar
5 ml ground mixed spice
250 ml wholewheat flour
200 ml seedless raisins
1 egg
60 ml milk
60 ml water
60 ml oil

TOPPING
milk
5 ml castor sugar
5 ml ground cardamom or cinnamon

Sift cake flour, baking powder, salt, sugar and spice. Add wholewheat flour and raisins and toss until coated. Whisk together egg, milk, water and oil. Pour into a well in centre of dry ingredients and, using a fork, mix to a soft dough. As soon as mixture holds together, pat out 2 cm thick on lightly floured board. Dough will be soft, therefore flour a 6 cm cutter before cutting out rounds. Place on oiled baking tray, brush with milk and sprinkle with combined sugar and spice. Bake just above centre of oven at 220 °C for 12 minutes.
Makes 12

Home-baking at its Best

Yeast Breads

Bread-baking is a long and involved story, dating right back to the Stone Age, when grain was crushed between two stones, mixed to a dough with water, shaped into thin cakes and baked on a stone over a fire. As can be imagined, these bread cakes were hard and very chewy. The triumph of discovering 'risen' bread is ascribed to a forgetful Egyptian, who mixed some dough and then went off somewhere on his camel, leaving the dough sitting in the hot sun – whereupon it fermented, and rose. Another, more plausible story, is that they learnt to use the yeasty foam from the top of their fermenting wines.

In due course the Egyptians grew so much wheat that they were able to export it. The Greeks bought much of the grain, and were so quick to develop the art of baking beautiful breads that they became the master bakers of the period. The skill was further developed by the conquering Romans, who eventually introduced their knowledge to Britain. It is said that Cassius was so appalled by the quality of the bread he found on his arrival in Britain, that he signalled his baker in Rome to send him some that he could eat.

It took many centuries before proper mills were developed and bread became a commodity within everyone's reach. Today, of course, due to mechanization, bread in all its forms is available everywhere.

Basically, bread is made from flour, yeast, salt and liquid, and kneading it allows the gluten in the flour to stretch and form an elastic framework around the gas bubbles from the yeast.

Flour: There are four main types of wheat flour available in this country for bread-baking. White bread flour is used for most white breads. It has a high gluten content, and produces loaves of a creamy colour. Cake flour is highly refined and produces finely textured, fluffy rolls; it may also be used for very light breads. Brown bread flour or meal has had the coarsest bran removed and produces light brown loaves with a good volume. Wholewheat flour or meal contains a high percentage of bran and wheat germ. Bread made from this flour is dark in colour, has a slightly nutty flavour and a dense coarse texture. Flours made from other grains, like rye, have very little gluten and should always be mixed with another flour. Soya flour is rich in protein, and helps bread to remain fresh and moist. Both with regard to rising times and the amount of water absorbed, please be prepared to adapt; there are few hard and fast rules and it really is a matter of trial and perception. Sometimes a dough will 'draw' together quickly into a ball – at other times you could add the same amount of water and find it looks flaky. Different flours vary in regard to absorption capacity, and this must be borne in mind. Nevertheless, yeast cookery should be tackled with confidence and enthusiasm. Short of not activating the yeast by using water that is too cool, or killing it with water that is too hot, if it is properly kneaded it will eventually spring up and do wonderful things for you.

Yeast: Yeast is a living substance composed of tiny cells. When provided with moisture, food and warmth, the cells grow and give off carbon dioxide, which causes the dough to rise. Yeast also gives off alcohol, which is driven off by the heat of the oven, but which can give the dough a sour taste if left to rise for too long. And please do not think that by using more yeast you will get a better rise – the bread will simply taste yeasty. Yeast should not be hurried and, given time, even relatively small quantities will rise heavy doughs.

For the sake of convenience, I have used dried yeast in all recipes requiring yeast. It is available in sachets as well as tins and, unlike compressed yeast, it keeps well – although once opened it is best to store it, sealed, in the refrigerator. Instant dry yeast is sold in 10 g-sachets. It has a long shelf life, but should be used right away once opened.

When dissolving dried yeast, the water temperature is most important. If it is too hot, the yeast cells will be killed; if too cold, they will not grow. A little warmer than lukewarm is about right, but experience remains the best teacher. A little sugar is usually added to the water as food for the yeast, and the yeast is then sprinkled on the surface. Do not stir, but leave it to froth, and then just before adding it to the flour, give it a quick stir to make sure that all the granules have dissolved.

Liquid: Water is, naturally, the easiest liquid to use and provides the best volume and will result in a thick, crisp crust. The addition of milk, however, will make the bread more nutritious and it also improves the texture of the crumb and results in a softer crust. I always scald the milk first, and then leave to cool to lukewarm – scalding destroys bacteria and makes the dough somewhat easier to handle. The amount of liquid added to a dough varies, depending on the type of flour used. Start with the specified amount, and if the dough appears flaky, make further small additions until the required elasticity is reached. Once kneaded, further liquid cannot be successfully added, although extra flour can be incorporated into a too-soft dough.

Salt: Bread without salt is not palatable, but it should be used with discretion. Salt prevents the yeast from fermenting too quickly, thereby providing a good texture due to a slower rising, but too much of it will kill the yeast and then it won't rise at all. Too little salt results in a coarse crumb.

MILL

Sugar: Apart from being a food for the yeast, sugar also gives colour to the crust. Because it slows down the fermentation process, sweet yeast loaves require a longer rising period than plain breads. Remember that too much sugar will produce a poorly risen loaf.

Shortening: Butter, margarine or lard are regarded as the best shortenings for improving keeping qualities, increasing volume, and adding to the flavour and softness of crumb. Oil may also be used, especially in the baking of 'health' breads, but it does nothing for the colour of the loaf.

Eggs: These are sometimes added to enrich and colour bread. Breads containing eggs also have a much more tender crust.

Dried fruit, cheese, vegetables: The addition of these makes the dough heavier and involves a longer rising period.

Kneading: Turn the dough out onto a lightly floured board and be prepared for a ten-minute session. I do not think one can ever over-knead a dough, and under-kneading will have an undesirable result – so roll up your sleeves and punch away. The idea is to fold the dough over and then push it down and away with the heels of your palms; turn it slightly – I find an anti-clockwise movement comes most naturally – and then fold and press down again. On and on. It becomes quite hypnotic eventually, especially when the dough starts responding by becoming smooth and soft and pliable, without being sticky. If it does feel sticky, sprinkle a little extra flour on the board and carry on – if necessary sprinkle on more flour, but do so a little at a time so that you don't make the dough too stiff, in which case it cannot 'balloon'.

Rising: In order to avoid a crust forming on top of the dough, brush the mixing bowl with oil, turn the dough in it to coat the top, then cover. Another method is to cover the bowl with a damp cloth. The dough is then left to rise in a warm, draught-free place. Rising times vary, depending on the temperature in your kitchen – in cold weather it will, of course, take longer. Rising times are also affected by the amount of yeast, the kind of flour, and the extra ingredients used. I like to put the bowl in the warming drawer of my oven. Switch it on briefly beforehand and then switch it off again. If the dough is allowed to get too hot, the bread will be coarse and will break. As a general rule, the dough should double in volume. If allowed to over-prove, the loaf will have a coarse texture and poor flavour, while under-proving produces a heavy loaf with a loose top.

Second rising or proving: Once doubled, punch the dough down by pushing your fist into the middle, turn it inwards and over, and knead again for a minute or two to break up the pockets of gas. For really fine-textured bread, it may be left to rise again – but this is time-consuming. Alternatively, either shape the dough immediately, or better still, cover and let it rest for ten minutes, and then shape and cover. Oiled plastic wrap is convenient because it does not lie heavily on the dough. Do not cover tightly – leave space for air to circulate. Leave to rise until doubled, or nearly doubled in some cases, once again in a warming drawer or other warm spot.

Glazing: This is usually done just before baking and, although egg-wash is often recommended, especially when baking rolls, I usually use milk – breaking an egg just for glazing seems an unnecessary extravagance and milk or water or a sugar-water solution are all satisfactory. Coarsely crushed wheat, sesame, sunflower or poppy seeds make attractive finishes. With certain breads or rolls a pan of boiling water may be placed on the bottom shelf of the oven to encourage a shiny, crisp crust.

Baking: Even with sweet breads, which are usually baked at lower temperatures, I like to start off with a hot oven in order to stop the fermentation of the yeast. Exact temperatures and positioning in the oven are specified with each recipe – it is important to abide by them to avoid over-browning. To test whether a loaf (or a roll) is done, turn it over and knock on the bottom – it should sound distinctly hollow. If in doubt, return to the oven, out of the tin and upside down, for a short while at a lower temperature. Always cool bread completely on a wire rack before storing.

Mishaps: Here again experience is the best teacher and the more you bake with yeast the sooner you will learn the reason for imperfect results and how to avoid them. However, a few pointers may help. The greatest mistakes are in making a dough too wet or too dry, under- or over-proving, and insufficient kneading. These will result in loaves that have poor volume, an uneven shape, heavy texture, holes and a coarse crumb, with a crust that either breaks at the sides, or is very thick and has a poor crumb colour. Over-risen dough, especially in too warm a place, also results in a strong yeast taste. Using a tin of the wrong size also spells disaster to the shape of a loaf – if the tin is too small you'll end up with an irregular shape and a cracked crust. Frankly, there's such a long list of possible faults that it is best just to follow the recipes carefully, remembering the main points I have listed, and the importance of the correct temperature – both in dissolving the yeast, rising and proving, and finally, in baking.

Shaping breads: The traditional loaf tin bread has great appeal. Press the dough into a rectangle and then fold inwards from each side. Drop into the tin with the seam underneath. A farmhouse-style loaf may be made by slashing the top lengthwise, creating a sunburst effect. Plaits or braids are also most effective – divide the dough into three, roll into sausages and plait – but not too tightly. Cobs are made by shaping the dough into a round ball, then flattening it slightly before placing on a floured sheet, proving and then sprinkling the top with flour before baking. Cottage loaves are made in the same way as cottage rolls, but are larger. A bloomer loaf is a long loaf with blunt ends and a flat top, fatter than a French loaf, and slashed on top before proving. When proving these loaves, which are not placed in tins, it is a good idea to support the sides with crumpled dish cloths so that they do not spread sideways too much. Tins other than loaf tins may be used, such as tube tins, or round cake tins, as in crown loaves. These are amongst the most attractive of breads: the dough is shaped into rolls, and arranged round the circumference of the tin, with one roll in the middle. They are then topped with grated cheese, sesame or poppy seeds. In proving and baking, these rolls join to form a 'crown' of humped buns.

Sweet Yeast Breads

Although these are not as straightforward as regular breads, they are fun to make, especially with an eye to shapes and decorations. I have included a few recipes, mostly of Continental origin, where they are most popular. Due to the addition of 'heavy' ingredients they will take longer to rise and prove, and although they are usually baked at a lower temperature because they brown more quickly, I like to start them off at a high temperature, as I said, to kill the yeast, and then reduce the temperature after about 10 minutes. They are usually baked towards the top of the oven. Sweet yeast breads may either be decorated before baking, or left to cool, and simply iced. They stale quite quickly, and may then be toasted.

Rolls

These are usually baked at a high temperature towards the top of the oven, and eaten fresh. Experimenting with different shapes can be really rewarding. The most common are round rolls; sausage-shaped finger rolls; snails, twists and knots – which are made by first rolling the dough into long thin sausages; cottage rolls, in which a small ball of dough is placed on top of a larger round and secured by pushing your finger through the centre; and crescents, which, like croissants, are shaped by rolling a triangle up from the long end and twisting into a horseshoe.

Rusks

I have included kneaded rusks and 'easy' rusks – both good and lovely for dunking. It is important, when separating rusks, not to slice them as this does affect the flavour. It is fine to use a knife as an aid, but it is better to use the tines of a fork. Whatever you do, always try to break them through, and dry them out on baking trays in a very low oven or warming drawer so that they end up crisped without browning.

Quick Breads

Whether sweet or savoury, these are great time-savers and require no rising times as they are made with self-raising flour, baking powder, or bicarbonate of soda and cream of tartar. Cheese and/or nuts are often used in these loaves, and it is useful to have a ready-grated or chopped supply available. I grate large quantities of cheese in my food processor, using the grinding blade, and then store it in plastic bags in my freezer. The same applies to nuts, but be careful not to grind too them finely, otherwise the end-product will not have the same texture. Sweet quick loaves are often more flavoursome if left for a day or two before slicing.

Scones

It goes without saying that scones should always be eaten fresh. They are baked at a high temperature, towards the top of the oven. It is preferable not to roll them out before cutting – patting is better – to ensure lightness, and if using a cutter, be sure not to twist as you cut, as they will not rise as they should. A dash of lemon juice will also help to lighten scones.

Muffins

The golden rule here is never to overmix; muffin batter will usually be lumpy rather than smooth. Never over-fill tins as they will rise over the sides and be difficult to remove. As with scones, break, rather than slice them in half before buttering.

Biscuits

I have tried to keep the time expended in biscuit-making to a minimum because few of us, these days, can indulge in rolling and cutting and baking tray after tray of biscuits as they used to do in granny's day, so I have included many recipes for biscuits that are simply rolled into balls. There are also some refrigerator biscuits, which only need to be sliced once chilled, and bar biscuits, which are especially convenient when it comes to speed – but do try to use the size of tin recommended so that the biscuits are neither too thick nor too thin. (Incidentally, the term 'biscuit' used to be reserved for a dry, twice-baked, flour and water mixture, but today, cookies – which are quite different in texture and flavour – are also called biscuits.) Using soft (not melted) butter when creaming a biscuit mixture will make the job much easier and will ensure successful results. Insufficient creaming can result in a mixture that is too dry to shape, so here again the electric beater comes in useful.

Shortening: I have introduced several recipes using oil instead of butter to cope with differing tastes and budgets. This will also make them more suitable for low-cholesterol diets. These biscuits are sometimes more difficult to handle, but are well worth attempting, and are often the crispest and most economical. I also find oil best for greasing tins and trays for all baking. Whenever possible, and especially in the case of biscuits rich in butter, position the trays on the middle shelf of the oven, to avoid over-browning on the bottom; if time allows, it is therefore better to bake biscuits in relays. Certain nutritious and unrefined ingredients have been introduced in several recipes, because it has been my experience that these are becoming increasingly popular, especially with teenagers.

Storing: Once cooled on wire racks, biscuits should be stored in airtight containers. It is a good idea, in the case of crisp biscuits, to sprinkle each layer with a little sugar to keep them crunchy.

Index